THE RIDDLE OF THE EXODUS

The Riddle of the Exodus

First Printing 4/2002

Published by Lightcatcher Books

842 Kissinger Ave.
Springdale, Arkansas 72762
www.lightcatcherprod.com

ISBN 0-9719388-0-6

TABLE OF CONTENTS

Chapter Five

Chapter Six

Chapter Seven

Chapter Eight

Section Three -- Leaving Egypt

Chapter Nine

Chapter Ten

Chapter Eleven

Acknowledgments

Without hesitation I thank God for allowing me the opportunity to write this book. The Creator has surely introduced me to some very special people who have aided and abetted me in this endeavor. I owe a debt of gratitude to the work of Paul Rothstein whose research I literally stumbled onto years ago. During one of my first trips to Israel, Rabbi Avraham Sutton would finally introduce me to Mr. Rothstein. Rabbi Sutton has also been a wonderful teacher and the warmest of friends. I must also express my appreciation to author and linguist Isaac Mozeson who graciously agreed to edit this manuscript, offering salient and witty critiques. I hope some of his brilliance has touched this work. I want to thank Professor Vendyl Jones for introducing me to the wonders and the riches of the Torah. His reputation for being a renegade does not diminish the impact of his efforts to foster an understanding of Judaism, the Jewish People and their vital role as God's Chosen People. Finally, I am eternally grateful to my wife, Carol, who pressed me with loving encouragement to actually do this thing. Her considerable talents can be seen in the layout and format of this book, even the cover design. Carol has been a partner from start to finish.

A Word About the Biblical Quotations

Any translator of Biblical Hebrew will tell you that most English renderings fall short of transmitting the richness and depth of the original Hebrew text. But some translations are better than others. I have chosen to quote the scripture from the Five Books of Moses as found in *The Living Torah* translated by the late Aryeh Kaplan. Other Biblical verses come from *The Living 'Nach*. Both texts are available from Maznaim Publishing Corporation in New York.

I would also like to alert readers unfamiliar with the Hebrew Bible that the numbering of passages in the Hebrew is sometimes different from that of the English versions.

INTRODUCTION

The Passover That Never Was

I have always believed that the Exodus happened. Blame it on Cecil B. DeMille and his Paramount epic *The Ten Commandments*. The narrative and accompanying visual spectacle had an undeniable impact on my then eight-year-old mind. Viewing *The Ten Commandments* as an adult I had to chuckle at its creaky directing style and stilted, operatic performances that were old-fashioned even by Hollywood standards of 1956. Years later, I would stand where Moses supposedly stood. I was on Jebel Syagha, in Jordan, looking towards Israel. Siyagha is the highest point on the Nebo range of mountains and thought to be *Pisgah* (Hebrew for "peak"), the site where Moses viewed the Promised Land. Deuteronomy relates that Moses could see all the way from "Dan to Beersheba" a panorama that encompassed a region roughly 50 miles wide, from east to west and running approximately 165 miles from north to south. Of course, I could see far less as I squinted through that smoky veil of pollution. It now seems to me something else has also clouded modern man's view of that momentous epic.

These days, professing belief in the Biblical account of Israel's miraculous redemption by God is very often met with outright ridicule. This situation reached its nadir when a Los Angeles rabbi told the press that there was not one shred of evidence to prove the Exodus had actually occurred. And he chose the Passover season to announce this to the world. My first thought was to contact my close observant Jewish acquaintances in Israel and tell them that there was no reason to rid the house of *chametz,* to put away the *matzah* and forget about answering the four questions posed by Jewish children for centuries on *Pessach.*[1] Why bother, since a newspaper story had banished Moses to the realm of myth populated by Santa Claus and the Easter Bunny.

How could this be? Why would a son of Israel, in one glib proclamation, wipe out thousands of years of history? To accept his words would render the whole Passover Feast empty and artificial, if not null and void.[2] To me, that act was tantamount to one of our U.S. congressmen stating that the founding of America and the signing of the Declaration of Independence was much embellished by legend. The skeptic might counter that while we can offer the aforementioned document as proof of America's beginnings, no such evidence exists for the Exodus account.

We do possess testimony that is ancient and unchanged. I would also add that it served the same noble purpose as the legal instrument drafted by our forefathers. I am referring to The Torah, the so-called Five Books of Moses. For the Jewish People it is their Declaration of Independence, Bill of Rights and Title Deed to the Land of Israel all literally rolled into one.

God did something at Sinai that was unique in human history. He created a nation. Every country since time immemorial has emerged from migration, war, conquest or human mandate. Israel is the only nation formed by and under the auspices of the Creator of time and space. By declaring this I have immediately positioned myself as an extremist on the subject for I have stumbled from the straight and narrow of science to the intangible regions of faith.

I have not written this book for those happy in the conceit that everything taught by the rank and file of archaeology is the truth and cannot be challenged. I have undertaken this task ever since I discovered that the whole study of antiquity is simply a house of theoretical cards built on shaky ground. It is a modern framework superimposed on the span of the centuries that is ill fitting and often incomprehensible.

This work is for those who have searched for answers in publications like *Biblical Archaeological Review* and found it a maddening experience. Every new disclosure of evidence that might broaden our view of the Bible's historical aspects is met with howling rebuttal. Men of science will remind us that this is the acid test of peer review that allows discoveries to be granted a seal of approval—but the seal is never granted.

A prime example is Tel Jericho, a site that possesses a genuine Biblical pedigree. It meets the geographic criteria of the scriptural narrative and the excavated remains exhibit all the signs of a city demolished just as described in the book of Joshua. Most scholars still maintain that the armies of Israel never destroyed Jericho. The late British archaeologist Kathleen Kenyon was the foremost proponent of this view. She believed that the ruins at Jericho could not be dated to correspond with Israel's entry into the land. However, her thesis was faulty from the beginning. Kenyon's proposed date of this event was pure conjecture and her conclusions were based not on what she found,

--but what she did not find at Jericho![3] Those who march lockstep with Ms. Kenyon have created an archaeological maze further complicated by a dating system that is terribly flawed.

Let us turn our attention to ancient Egypt during the time that the Exodus saga unfolded. Surely, an empire so terribly impacted by this event should have record of it. While the official line maintained by the archaeological community dismisses the Exodus tale, scholars (without realizing it) actually come to conclusions that harmonize with the Biblical record. In the study of Egypt and the Exodus there are certain facts that are hard to dispute.

Riddle of the Exodus is the culmination of over four years of research that I had done for my television documentary of the same name. This is important to remember because, by virtue of my profession, I am a researcher, who works with experts. Though I am not a card-carrying archaeologist that does not hinder me from being able to observe, analyze and marshal data into what I hope is a coherent readable work. And I am not an archaeologist in the contemporary meaning of the word. I could lay claim to that title as it was originally coined in 1607. As late as 1879 the word was defined as a science that, **"investigates by studying oral traditions, monuments of all kinds, and written manuscripts..."**[4]

Much of what we know (or think we know) about ancient Egypt is still a matter of conjecture and that is why the conclusions offered in this book are just as relevant as those held sacrosanct by most academics. Egyptology and Archaeology have yielded some tangible but very broad facts. But we must be vigilant for speculation passed off as fact. John Anthony West, a controversial figure in Egyptology, provides some insight into the official view of a field he describes as,

> "...in a state of constant ferment and revision, though the outsider would never suspect it."[5]

As an outsider, I would offer the reader a very radical thesis: the Exodus did not take place in the New Kingdom era of Rameses. Nor did it occur in the earlier Middle Kingdom during the time of the Hyksos, the so-called Shepherd Kings. By going to the ancient Jewish sources we find tantalizing clues that take us farther back in time, directly to the end of the Sixth Dynasty during the waning days of the Old Kingdom, an era that Bible scholars have completely ignored in their search for the Exodus. In the Old Kingdom we discover Pharaoh Neferkare Phiops II who ruled longer than any king in Egyptian history. He was succeeded by his son Neferkare the Younger who was followed by the first woman ruler of Egypt. What we can learn from the time of these three monarchs matches the account found in the Jewish Midrash known as *Sefer Ha Yashar*.

A striking parallel can be drawn from the Egyptian reports of the Old Kingdom's rapid demise. It came to an abrupt close during the reign of Neferkare the Younger. Literally overnight, the powerful Egyptian empire was brought to its knees and chaos was the norm for hundreds of years. Though Egyptologists cannot agree on the reasons for this descent into calamity, the Biblical narrative offers a compelling answer in its graphic description of disastrous plagues, the demise of the first-born, the primogeniture-privileged class, the loss of their elite cavalry and charioteers and an exiting labor force.

You would rightly ask how a drama of such scope could be missing from the Egyptian annals? Yet, a tattered document from the final chaotic days of the Sixth Dynasty known as *The Admonitions of an Egyptian Sage* challenges the view that the Egyptians kept no record of the Exodus and its profound impact. The description of disasters closely parallels the Biblical record in a manner that is both intellectually astonishing and personally heartbreaking.

What of the most dramatic event of all, the crossing of the Sea of Reeds?[6] A journey to the Egyptian town of Ismailia will lead to a local museum that houses a nearly forgotten artifact. It is a black granite monument covered in hieroglyphs that recounts the drowning of pharaoh's army—from the Egyptian point of view.

If the Exodus had never happened...if millions of Hebrew slaves, accompanied by a mixed multitude, had not departed Egypt in the wake of signs and wonders and if they had not received the Torah at Mount Sinai then there would be no Jewish People. You don't need a degree in theology to understand the further ramifications. Without the Jew and his Torah there would be no Christianity or Islam. Even though the Pentateuch is part of the canon of the Christian Old Testament some ministers will preach that the New Testament has replaced or "fulfilled" it. The Moslem cleric will similarly insist that the Koran is the final revelation given to Mohammed. But they cannot deny the basic historicity from Adam to Joshua as being the first revelation from the Creator. For millions of Jews and

Christians, the book of Exodus is an accurate chronicle that details the release of the ancient Hebrews from years of harsh Egyptian bondage and their eventual birth as the nation of Israel who would be obliged to a non-human taskmaster and laws largely grounded in this historical liberation.

The Exodus experience is rooted at the very core of Judaism. If modern Israel and the somehow still existent Jewish people are to fulfill their manifest destiny as a Light to the Nations then they must believe that their destiny was formed in the crucible of the Exodus and that it was every bit as authentic as the founding of the United States.

NOTES to Introduction

[1] In preparation for Passover, the entire house must be rid of any trace of *chametz* or leavening, whether on the floors or in food products. The four questions are actually in response to another question, "Why is this night different than all other nights?" (a)Why on this night do we only eat unleavend bread? (b)Why on this night do we only eat bitter herbs? (c)Why on this night do we dip them twice? (d)Why on this night do we recline?

[2] Ironically, the rabbi declared this from a synagogue called Temple *Sinai.*

[3] Bryant G. Wood, *Did the Israelites Conquer Jericho?* (Biblical Archaeological Review, Mar/April 1990)

[4] Barry Fell, *America B.C.* (Artisan Publishers, Muskogee, OK, 2001) p.30

[5] West, *Traveler's Key to Ancient Egypt* (Alfred A. Knopf, NY, 1988)p.xiii

[6] In the original Hebrew text, Israel crosses *Yam Suf*, Sea of Reeds

SECTION I
THE CONTROVERSY

CHAPTER ONE
Egyptology's Dirty Little Secrets

Despite lofty pronouncements from scholarly circles, Archaeology and Egyptology are really all about opinions. These disciplines actually shun ancient written sources as unreliable and too subjective. These same scholars will maintain that they offer the only objective view since their conclusions are based on hard evidence. Reporter Itamar Singer, writing in the Israeli newspaper *Ha'Aretz*, offers a clear-eyed assessment of such posturing.

> "If this were the case, there would be no bitter arguments among archaeologists over their interpretations of various findings. True, the silent remains do not lie but the archaeologists who speak in their name are no less subjective than the philologists who interpret the texts. Archaeology does not have the role of "supreme arbiter in the polemic on bible history, but is rather an active participant in the debate."[1]

The finds at Qumran are the purest example of archaeology fueled by an agenda. Witness the on-going controversy surrounding the Dead Sea Scrolls. Despite hundreds of scrolls and other relics, archaeologists still publish conflicting views of the site. For years the academicians from *Ecole Biblique* hoarded the precious scrolls claiming the texts were infused with the very origins of their church. Access granted other scholars in

1991 allowed the true Jewish character of the scrolls to be revealed.

One of the Dead Sea Scrolls on display at the Shrine of the Book in Jerusalem.

That sound you hear is derisive laughter issuing from the hallowed halls of academia. They are amused that someone so lacking in archaeological credentials would challenge their position. Do not misunderstand me; I am not opposed to scholarship. I am opposed to intellectual chauvinism parading as scholarship. John Anthony West is familiar with this curious mind-set that rejects any new concepts even when backed by solid scientific data.

> "To outsiders, the resistance to new and sound theories in scientific and scholarly disciplines is often incomprehensible, since these disciplines are ostensibly dedicated to the discovery of the objective truth…but in the case of the scholar or scientist, a sound theory that contradicts views held and pursued for a lifetime pulls the rug out from under his or her ego, and a familiar

> paradoxical situation develops. The people professionally engaged in discovering the "truth" are those psychologically least capable of accepting the "truth" if it happens to contradict what they already believe...Nowhere is this more apparent than in Egyptology."[2]

My point is this: I cannot conclusively prove my theories *but they cannot prove their theories either.* I can present you with data that is reasonably sound and offer my own interpretation. It is my hope that you will consider the evidence presented in this book and form your own conclusions based on the merit of that evidence—not my lack of credentials. Let's begin by looking at some of the problems that plague this discipline.

The Chronological Conundrum

In the more honest literary efforts of its practitioners, we sometimes learn that one of the most important tools utilized in Egyptology simply does not work. In the introduction to his *Pyramids of Egypt,* author I.E.S. Edwards spills the beans,

> "One of the first questions which occur to the mind of anyone looking at an ancient monument is its date. In the case of the Egyptian monuments it is often difficult, and sometimes impossible to answer the question in terms of years before the beginning of the Christian era, because our knowledge of Egyptian chronology is still very incomplete. We know the main sequence of events and frequently their relationship to one another, but, except in rare instances,

an exact chronology will not be possible until the discovery of material of a different and more precisely datable character than anything found hitherto."[3]

ANCIENT EGYPT

Periods	**Dynasties**
Archaic	PreDynastic
Early Dynastic	1st, 2nd, 3rd
Old Kingdom	4th, 5th, 6th
First Intermediate	7th, 8th, 9th, 10th
Middle Kingdom	11th, 12th
Second Intermediate	13th, 14th, 15th 16th, 17th (The Hyksos)
New Kingdom	18th, 19th, 20th
Third Intermediate	21st, 22nd, 23rd, 24th
Late Kingdom	25th, 26th 27th (Persian) 28th,29th, 30th
Second Persian	
Greco-Roman	Macedonian Kings Ptolemaic Roman Emperors Byzantine Emperors

Dr. Edwards is referring to the Egyptian Chronology. It is a timetable that encompasses the whole of ancient Egyptian history by charting each Pharaoh, his years on the throne and divides the whole business into thirty-one Dynasties. It is an amalgam drawn partly from a record set down by Manetho, an Egyptian priest who lived in the Third Century BCE. But his work only survives through second-hand sources such as the Jewish historian Flavius Josephus. Others who quote Manetho are Sextus Julius Africanus and Eusebius.[4] The use of this chronology is still very much a part of the study of ancient Egypt. As Sir Alan Gardiner noted,

> "In spite of all defects this division into dynasties has taken so firm a root in the literature of Egyptology that there is little chance of its ever being abandoned."[5]

The system is so pervasive that the uninitiated reader is often left with the impression that this is a method of recording history employed by the pharaohs and their scribes. If we could be transported back in time, to the streets of ancient *Menifir* (Memphis), and ask someone what Dynasty we were in, they would reply, "What's a Dynasty?"[6]

Archaeological discoveries such as the Kings List at Abydos, the Turin Papyrus, the Tables found at Saqqara and Karnak are all chronicles that reveal the basic order of the pharaohs and their reigns. When Manetho's list is compared to the Turin Papyrus we discover that these two separate chronicles are slightly at odds with each other. The table from Manetho reveals a total of forty-nine kings during the first six dynasties while the Turin document records fifty-two.

These flaws might be overlooked, especially if this timetable were utilized only as a general reference tool. However, the Egyptian Chronology contains a serious defect that is rarely acknowledged—nor has it been corrected. *No one can agree at what point in time that the chronology begins.* Since this chronology has been introduced it has been revised over twenty times! With each revision, the chronology has been severely reduced. Egyptologists have now decreased the span within the thirty-one dynasties by three thousand years.[7]

The Kings Gallery in the Temple at Abydos offers a nearly complete list of Egyptian rulers from the 1st to 19th Dynasty. The list was commissioned by Seti I.

There is a distinct possibility that some Egyptian Dynasties were co-existent rather than consecutive. For instance, in the Old Kingdom period, the pharaohs of Third, Fourth and Sxth Dynasties all ruled from Memphis. But the Fifth Dynasty kings held court at Elephantine near the southern border of ancient Egypt. This appears to be an odd shift back and forth between seats of power especially when we learn that, until the close of the Sixth Dynasty, much of this period in history was noted for its stability. However, the Elephantine kings could have been co-regents with their Memphite counterparts. That would explain what at first appears to be an anomalous shift between two ancient capitols.

The tiny figure of Fourth Dynasty pharaoh, Khufu, known to the Greeks as Cheops. This king is credited with building the Great Pyramid.

All Egyptologists agree that the Great Pyramid was built by the Fourth Dynasty Pharaoh Khufu (Cheops) but this is based on one cartouche containing his name found within the monument.

This creaky dating system is actually the handiwork of modern scholars. It is a contrivance that has resulted in a cross-pollination of various disciplines that contaminate each other with circular reasoning. I challenge the reader to pick up any book on ancient Egypt containing a list of pharaohs within the thirty-one dynasties and compare it with the same kind of table found in any other book on Egypt. None of these charts will match. Implementing this timetable has resulted in collateral damage that disrupts the entire dating system of Assyria, Babylon, Persian and even ancient Israel.

Though the defects in the Egyptian Chronology are critical, the field is plagued by other lapses. Among these problematic methods is Sothic Dating, one of Egyptology's favored parlor tricks.

Sirius Business

Once, in Jerusalem, I had an unforgettable encounter with a well-known Bible scholar. We both happened to be leasing cars at a small rental agency near the King David Hotel. I recognized him from his placid, bearded visage in the pages of *Biblical Archaeological Review.* While waiting for our paperwork to be processed, we struck up a conversation and the talk turned to our respective fields. When he asked about my work, I told him that I recently had come from Cairo where I was shooting footage for a documentary on the Exodus. As I shared my radical views, citing the end of the Old Kingdom being linked to the Exodus, the look of interest in his eyes began to retreat and his smile froze. His mental tuner was rapidly dialing out the sound of my voice. He stopped me with an upraised palm. The theologian insisted that the Egyptian Chronology did not allow for such a theory, that the chronology was set in stone and the proof of its worth was the Sothic dating. With that he collected his rental contract and his wife and drove away.

To ward off my evil influence, the good professor had chanted the holy mantra of Sothic dating. It attempts to fix a firm date for the beginning of the 18th Dynasty based on observing the heliacal rising of Sirius, the Dog Star, called Sothis by the Greeks. Somehow, using this system is supposed to allow us to align the ancient Egyptian civic calendar with the astronomical calendar (they only line up every 1450 years!) thus locking the whole of Egypt's history into an exact year-by year chronicle. Author Hilary Wilson relates this system is far from being set in stone.[8]

> "In the course of dynastic history, several scribes mentioned the occasion of the heliacal rising of Sirius but only once, as late as AD 139, was the absolute coincidence of the two calendars recorded. Calculating back in units of 1450 years, or thereabouts, this gives the possible date for the initiation of the civil calendar somewhere between 2780 and 2760 BC but since it was almost certainly in use before that date, another 1450 years back takes the creation of the Egyptian calendar into the predynastic age. On the papyrus from the temple at el-Lahun at the entrance to the Fayum, the heliacal rising of Sirius is said to have occurred on the 25th day of the first month of winter in the seventh year of the reign of Senusert III. This translates to a date around 1872 BC. This is one of the very few dates which modern Egyptologists have built their chronology."[9]

Am I the only one bothered by the liberal sprinkling of phrases like "or thereabouts, possible date or, a date of around," in the above explanation? We are supposed to be talking about fixed dates and exact alignments of calendars and constellations. Some breathing room is fine when pulling back the pages of the past because there are some things we just do not know. But people, like my Bible scholar friend, parades this flabby construct, called Sothic Dating, as if it were a precise mathematical model.

I suspect that the Bible scholar was simply spouting what I call dinner party data: casual information gleaned from other like-minded acquaintances. Since I am lower in the academic food chain, my viewpoint simply had no weight. Hopefully, the Sothic Calendar is falling out of fashion with honest practitioners. As for investigating the Sixth Dynasty, Sothic dating is useless for fixing events in the Old Kingdom era because at this juncture we do not have celestial data available from the Old Kingdom.

Like trying to unwrap a rotting mummy, the task of unraveling the secrets of ancient Egypt is complicated by a number of crumbling conventions instituted ages ago. They will not change them, treating them as sacrosanct and untouchable. I will have to bow to some of these conventions in some small measure but only as a general reference tool. In the previous pages my aim was to expose you to all of the various failings in the present system of study and to demonstrate that *we are still dealing with a very inexact field which parades whole theories as fact.* Again, I will quote John Anthony West who sums up this situation with this simple warning,

> "When it comes to Egyptian history, take whatever information you may be given with a pinch of salt and keep an open mind to conflicts of opinion. Beyond a reasonable certainty of the succession of the kings, very little that passes for Egyptian history is fact."[10]

Can You Speak Hieroglyph?

When you converse with someone on the streets of modern Cairo you speak Arabic. That has been the national tongue since the Moslems conquered the country centuries ago. Before that, the Byzantine Empire had swept in leading the nation into Christianity. The people spoke Egyptian but wrote using Greek script. The language was known as Coptic and it could still be heard in obscure pockets of the country as late as the 1930's.[11]

We can only speculate as to ancient character and sound of the ancient Egyptian tongue. The language survives only in three distinct forms: hieroglyphs,

The Rosetta Stone found near the village of Rashid by soldiers in Napolean's army. It would provide the key to translating hieroglyphs.

hieratic and demotic. The ability to read hieroglyphs had disappeared completely by 500 CE. Translating these obscure pictographs would not occur until centuries later. It began at Rashid with discovery of the Rosetta Stone by soldiers in Napoleon's army in 1799. In 1822, through the efforts of scholars such as a young French prodigy, Jean-Francois Champollion, the secrets of the hieroglyphs were unlocked.

Comprehending their meaning is one thing but verbalizing these signs is something we still wrestle with today. Part of the problem stems from an attribute common to the ancient Middle Eastern languages: *there were no vowels*.

Egyptologist Dr. Barbara Mertz, who has a genuine knack for clarifying the complexities of this discipline, explains.

> "Hieroglyphic writing expresses only consonants—and since hieratic and demotic are derived from hieroglyphs, the same is true of them. Therefore when Egyptologists transliterate Egyptian, they write a word with only the consonants. When students read the texts aloud in class, they follow the accepted practice of inserting an "e" between the consonants to facilitate articulation. If you listen to someone reading Egyptian aloud, following this convention, you will not hear Egyptian as spoken in the days of the pharaohs. The convention is allowed only because the true vocalization is still in doubt."[12]

With so many hieroglyphs at their disposal, it would appear that the ancient Egyptians had all of the

Hieroglyphs can be read one of three ways. The direction that the animal or human figures face will determine whether to read from the right or left, otherwise they are read from the top to the bottom.

phonetic bases covered. The language was actually limited to some degree. As far as we can determine, there was no "l" sound in the ancient Egyptian tongue so when they encountered that sound in foreign names or words the glyph representing the "r" sound was generally substituted or a compound of "rw". The letter translated as a "t" was rendered with a "d" hieroglyph.[13]

If we were to climb back into our imaginary time machine, warp back to ancient Thebes and ask directions to the palace of Pharaoh Thutmose the response would be a quick, "Pharaoh Who?" We should probably be asking for someone whose name sounds more like *Dhwty-nht*. How do you actually articulate a series of consonants when you really don't know which vowels to stick in between them? The name is also problematic for other reasons. The first element of the name, "thut" is from the Greek "thoth", the god of wisdom. "mose" is allegedly Egyptian meaning "son of".[14] The name Thutmose is actually a hybrid form, half Greek and half Egyptian created in some language lab. As John Anthony West points out, one of the difficulties in trying to uncover the mysteries of Egypt is the influence of the Greeks

> "While it is true that scholars today do not really know how ancient Egyptian was pronounced, the Greeks appear guilty of any number of etymological crimes, producing

The Greeks have had a profound effect on our study of ancient Egypt. The titles of the pharaohs and even the modern name of the country are from Greek.

"Cheops" out of *Khufu*, "Thoth" our of *Djehuti* and "Ozymandias" out of *User-maat-re*, at the same time causing almost inextricable confusion even among scholars, since certain Greek names, such as Memphis, have taken such prominence that the proper Egyptian names are seldom used, while in other cases the Egyptian name prevails and in still other cases, the Greek and Egyptians are freely interchanged."[15]

We cannot even discuss the monuments synonymous with Egypt without invoking the Greek.

For example, the word "pyramid" comes from Greek tourists who thought the massive triangular piles of stone resembled their own wheat cakes. The sky scraping "obelisks" reminded them of the spits on which they roasted meat.[16] Apparently, these first Ionian visitors were Epicureans since they seemed to equate everything with food. This Hellenizing of Egypt began with the arrival of the Ptolemaic line of rulers following the death of Alexander the Great. Naturally their influence has extended into every arena of Egypt's culture, including their pantheon of gods. Ever heard of the god called Wsir? You don't recognize the name because we all know the deity by his Greek name Osiris.

Even though historians and archaeologists appear to favor the Greek sources, they are reluctant to acknowledge the Biblical influence on their respective fields. The word "pharaoh" is a perfect example. The word is allegedly derived from the Egyptian *perah* translated as "great house". Supposedly *perah* was employed in the same way we use "the White House" when referring to presidential matters. Egyptologist Alan Gardiner stated that "pharaoh" was drawn directly from the Bible but that the word was "picked up by the writers of the scriptures..."and is really an anachronism.[17] But I wonder. If we look at the Hebrew root of "pharaoh", we find a connection to Egypt's ancient religion.

Holy Cow

In 1850, Auguste Mariette discovered a site called the Serapeum, near ancient Memphis. This was an underground burial chamber for the Apis Bulls. It still ranks as one of the great discoveries of Egyptology.

Worship of the bull can be traced to the very earliest period of Egypt's history.

The worship of their blessed bovine was practiced from the First Dynasty down through the centuries, even into the later era of the Ptolemaic rulers of Egypt. A young bull, completely black, except for special markings on its forehead, was honored as the Apis Bull. Upon its death the animal was mummified and interred with great ceremony. The pharaoh was the personification of this bull and its traits.

> "The early dynastic kings were frequently shown as bulls and it would appear that for political reasons they adopted the bull cult of the north, particularly Apis who perhaps existed long before the first king of united Egypt."[18]

In the Hebrew of the Torah, the word pharaoh is closely related to the word *parah* which means cow.[19] The Torah may be alluding to this ancient practice of the king being personified as a bull. The link between the deified Egyptian king and the cow is demonstrated in Genesis, Chapter 41 when the king, in Joseph's time, experiences a prophetical dream. Seven years of plenty and seven years of famine are symbolized in the ruler's dream as cattle coming from the depths of the Nile. Pharaoh's dream reveals the Egyptian cosmology in which the sacred Nile and the sacred cow are associated with the pharaoh himself.

A linguist might take exception to linking the Hebrew *parah* and "pharaoh." They would rightfully explain that the Hebrew word for bull is *shor*. The affinity between the ancient Egyptian and Hebrew could allow for this association. After all, the general term for the animal whether male or female is still a cow.[20] The ritual of the Apis bull immediately brings to mind the episode of the Golden Calf in Chapter 32 of the book of Exodus.

> "God declared to Moses, 'Go down, for the people whom you brought out of Egypt have become corrupt. They have been quick to leave the way that I ordered them to follow, and they have made themselves a cast-metal calf. They have bowed down and offered sacrifice to it, exclaiming, 'This, Israel, is your god, who brought you out of Egypt.'" - Exodus 32:7-8

Notes on Chapter One

[1] Singer, *The Bible as History?* (Ha'Aretz , December 28, 2001) .p B6

[2] West, *The Traveler's Key to Ancient Egypt*, p. 39 (Alfred A. Knopf 1988)

[3] Edwards, *The Pyramids of Egypt*, p.11 (Viking Press 1971)

[4] Manetho's *History of Egypt* was lost when Julius Caesar accidentally torched the famous Alexandrian Library in 4 7 BCE.

[5] See Gardiner's *Egypt of the Pharaohs*, p.46 (Oxford University Press 1961)

[6] The Egyptians were notorious for having several calendars

[7] Ezra, *Review of Ancient History*, p.3 (Jerusalem)

[8] David Rohl, Pharaohs and Kings (Crown Publishers 1995) pp.390-391

[9] Hilary Wilson, *Understanding Hieroglyphs*, (Michael O'Mara Books 1995) p.177

[10] West, *The Travelers Key to Ancient Egypt* (Alfred A. Knopf, NY, 1988) p.7

[11] Barbara Mertz, *Temples, Tombs and Hieroglyphs*, (Peter Bedrick Books 1990) pp.253-234

[12] Ibid, p. 255

[13] Hilary Wilson, *Understanding Hieroglyphs*, (Michael O'Mara Books Ltd. 1995) p.32

[14] Of course, the Bible in Exodus relates that "Moses" was Egyptian for "drawn from water."

[15] West, *The Traveler's Key to Ancient Egypt* (Alfred A. Knopf, New York, 1988) p.195

[16] Sir Alan Gardiner, *Egypt of the Pharaohs* (Oxford University Press 1961) p.2

[17] ibid, p.52

[18] W.B. Emery, ***Archaic Egypt*** (Penguin Books 1961) p.124

[19] By adding the letter "ayin" to "parah"

[20] Linguist Isaac Mozeson points out that *shor* really refers to oxen. *Shor* later morphed into the Latin *taurus* and Spanish *tauro*.

CHAPTER TWO

Why Ask the Chinese About the Irish?

The catalyst for my documentary and this book really began in 1994 when I came across a compact little tome entitled *Review of History*. Within its unwieldy subtitle, "A Plea for the Revision of Egyptian Chronology (And the Chronology of Other Peoples Based on Jewish Tradition)," I found a gleaming revelation. Paul Rothstein was the author of the treatise. He is a French Jew who had made *aliyah* to Israel after surviving the Holocaust. He now lives at Telz Stone, a quiet religious *yeshuv* nestled in the hills northwest of Jerusalem. He wrote under the name of Ezra, which comes from the Hebrew word for "help." In the introduction of Mr. Rothstein's simple but profound thesis, I realized why historians had failed to unlock this mystery surrounding the Exodus.

> "It is almost axiomatic to think of ancient history as having long preceded the history of Israel; Egypt is often depicted as being "eternal". It is generally unknown that the chronology of Judaism has remained virtually unchanged since its origins. Jewish Chronology therefore differs from secular chronology; the latter is subject to continual change. The Hebrew people, who have lived through ALL civilizations, have kept their memory alive—by their festivals."[1]

It was Mr. Rothstein's respect for his rich Jewish legacy that made me realize why the trail had often gone cold in my attempts to answer the riddle of the Exodus. Here was the reason why entire ranks of scholars were blindly leading others through the haze of history but continually stumbling along the way. ***In their arrogance they had chosen to ignore the ancient Jewish records.***

Here was the reason why entire ranks of scholars were blindly leading others through the haze of history but continually stumbling along the way. *In their arrogance they had chosen to ignore the ancient Jewish records.*

If historians do bother to mention such sources their remarks are dismissive at best. This is tantamount to writing about the origins of China but tossing out anything the Chinese might offer from their own ancient records. The very same situation has hindered the study of ancient Egypt for so many centuries. Scholars have depended heavily on the Greek accounts of Egypt's antiquity.

There is an extensive body of Egyptian history but much of it comes from the Greeks, beginning around 500 BCE with Hecataeus of Miletus.

The best known is Herodotus of Halicarnassus (484-430 BCE). We can add to this list Plato, along with Diodorus Siculus and Strabo. As Egyptologist Sir Alan

Gardiner suggests, as in the case of Herodotus, we can look to these Greek historians but not on all matters,

> "His account of the older Egyptian monarchy is deplorable, though he knew of Min (Menes) as its initiator. Also he was able to give in only slightly distorted form the names of the builders of Giza, namely Cheops, Chepheren and Mycerinos. Wildly wrong, however, was his placing before these, instead of after them, of a king Sesostris who is a conflation of several hundred rulers named Senwosre belonging to Manetho's Dynasty XII, and whose conquests, exaggerated out of all proportion…"[2]

The Greek historians were hindered in some measure because they were passing along second hand information. None of them could read hieroglyphs. In fact, by the fourth century, *no one* could read any of the ancient Egyptian texts or monuments since the ability to comprehend hieroglyphs, even by Egyptians, was a lost art. The impact of the Greeks is demonstrated in the name we still attach to this country. It is from the Greek *Aigyptos*. Gardiner believes that the word might be a Hellenistic corruption of *Hikupta*, an early alternate name for Memphis, the famous capital near the Nile Delta.[3]

The Mesopotamians knew Egypt as *Musur* or *Metsr*; which is closely related to *Mitzraim*, from the Hebrew. The latter is the Biblical founder Egypt. The ancient Egyptians referred to Egypt, in their native tongue, as *Kham* or *Khan* (the black land). Even this word points to the Biblical record. Ham (pronounced with a gutteral, hard 'h') was the grandfather of Mitzraim.[4]

In writing his *Review of History*, author Rothstein constructed his plea for the truth of the Exodus by not ignoring the Greeks but by regarding them as an ancillary source. He decided to look first to the honored histories of his ancestors guarded for thousands of years in the form of the *Tanakh* and other revered Jewish texts. If through the centuries, the *Chazal* (Jewish Sages) continued to transmit their unique perspective of an event that formed the very bedrock of their origins how can we deny the impact of that event? *In a politically correct world that continually waves the banner of diversity in our faces how can we fail to grant the Jews the relevance of their own heritage*?

Chapter Two Notes

[1] Paul Rothstein, *Revision of History*, (Jerusalem 1986)

[8] ibid, pp. 3-4

[3] Still, we cannot escape the Greek. Memphis is the Greek variant of Menefir (beautiful place).The Grecian form of names extends to many other ancient sites and the names of most pharaohs.

[4] Genesis 10:6

CHAPTER THREE
Help From Ezra

After reading his *Review of History*, I decided I had to interview Paul Rothstein for the project. Thanks to my good friend, Avraham Sutton, a brilliant writer in his own right, I was able to accomplish this meeting with little effort. Through what some might call serendipity, I learned that Mr. Rothstein actually lived

The author with historian Paul Rothstein at his home in Israel taking a break from videotaping an interview for Riddle of the Exodus.

up the street from Avraham in *Telz Stone*. Mr. Rothstein spoke only fluent Hebrew and of course, French. I comprehend enough of both languages to find my way through a menu, but Avraham, a former native of

Los Angeles, had been in Israel long enough to master *Ivrit* so he translated for both of us.

I interviewed Rothstein in his cramped study filled with histories from the classical and sacred sources. He sat next to stacks of meticulous charts and timetables rendered in his own precise hand. On the wall were his curious paintings that incorporated kabbalistic imagery and historical motifs in detailed, draftsman-like style.

I was to spend a total of eight hours with him spread across two videotaping sessions. Mr. Rothstein's quiet demeanor and the generous manner in which he shared his years of research convinced me that I was in the presence of a true sage of Israel.

His thesis was simple. Rothstein sought to find parallels between the Jewish account of the Exodus and corresponding events in Egyptian history. He first establishes what constitutes his main Jewish sources as the following:

- **The Hebrew Bible or Tanakh**. This source encompasses the Torah, the so-called Five Books of Moses. Every observant Jew believes that the written Torah was dictated to Moses by the Creator on Mt. Sinai along with the Oral Torah. The written Torah and Oral Torah are so intertwined that studying the written Torah without its Oral counterpart has been likened to missing the lecture and only reading the notes from it. Also in the *Tanakh* are the Prophets and Sacred Writings. This canon is nearly the same as the Christian Old Testament.[1]

■ **The Talmud**. Comprehensive and exhaustive, the Talmud is made up of the *Gemara* and the *Mishna*. The *Mishna* is a distillation of the Oral Torah. From this came the *Gemara,* which is a collection of records and legal discourses.

■ **Midrash**. The works of the *Midrash,* compiled by the Sages (the *Tannaim*), around 200 BCE. The *Midrash* contains a wealth of legendary material and parabolic texts.

■ **Seder Ha Olam.** This is the Chronology of the Jewish people. It dates every monumental event in Jewish history and the history of the world. It was set down by Rabbi Jose ben Halafta, sometime during the Second Century of the Common Era.

A Stack of Bibles

The Biblical account of history is widely discounted by the minimalists for one reason: The Bible is a "Holy" book. Being a sacred text somehow disqualifies it as history. The historical value is also dismissed because the Biblical text often recounts miracles. Professor Alan Millard takes the minimalists to task for their myopic standards.

> "Such narratives are not 'real history', we are told. Applying modern criteria to an ancient document is improper, however; the text needs to be evaluated in its context... that means looking at miracle stories in other ancient Near Eastern texts."[2]

The Egyptian and Assyrian records are ripe with accounts of victories ascribed to the intervention of their gods. The annals of Ashurbanipal record that when he was under siege, the gods of Assyria sent thunderbolts upon the enemy camp. The attackers were forced to withdraw from his frontier. The royal chronicles of Pharaoh Rameses II relate how the king prayed to Set to harness the elements to insure the safe delivery of his Hittite bride-to-be. Rameses memorialized what he considered to be a miracle claiming that his god caused summer-like weather to occur during the winter allowing his bride-to-be to arrive intact.[3] When other ancient peoples boast of higher powers aiding and abetting their faithful, scholars do not question the veracity of the event. The scholar might think it quaint but accepts these commemorations as cultural coloring.

However, if we are bold enough to make references to the Biblical sources one is liable to hear one of two scholarly rebukes: (1) the Bible cannot be taken literally and (2) the Biblical text can be used to prove anything.

My first response would be that something can be true without being taking literally. For example, the Torah commands, "an eye for an eye". This concept is the basis for our laws of compensatory damages. The value given must equal the value of the loss. However, the passage cannot be taken literally in the sense that plucking out the eye of the offending party would only cause additional harm. Most importantly it would prove a waste of time if the offending party were already blind!

As for the second complaint of our minimalists, I would lay the very same charge at their door. When artifacts are uncovered from other cultures that echo Biblical events, they arbitrarily decide, without any precedent, that the Hebrews absorbed or copied the event into their "myths." In this regard I would cite the famous Gilgamesh Tablet.

We are supposed to believe that the Hebrews copied the story of the Great Flood from this artifact since it is older than the oldest Torah scroll. Perhaps, but we will never find a Torah scroll older than the Gilgamesh Tablet because the Torah was given long after the Gilgamesh tablets were inscribed. If we are to doubt the legitimacy of the Torah because it was written long after the events it records then we must apply this same standard to the Gilgamesh artifact since it is supposedly a record of events long after they have occurred.

To solve the riddles of the Exodus we must allow that the Torah has some merit as an historical record. The so-called Higher Critics will argue that the Torah was written at a much later date in history. However, recent discoveries confirm that the Torah is much older than its detractors would have us believe. Before we continue with our search for answers to the Riddle of the Exodus, I want us to consider just one example of recent archaeological finds that call into the question the claims of the critics who believe the Bible is simply a collection of borrowed legends.

Seal of Approval

Artifacts are usually found as the result lengthy research mixed with a considerable amount of sweat from an archaeological dig. Sometimes they are rescued from an antiquities dealer. In 1975, a collection of *bullae* or clay seals was recovered from that very source. The value of those seals was greatly enhanced when more seals from the same time period were found during an excavation in Jerusalem by archaeologist Yigal Shiloh.

These are the smallest of artifacts but their weight on Israel's periodic chart of history is impressive. Some of the seals were the property of Gemariah, son of Shaphan. Another belonged to Baruch ben Neirah, the faithful secretary to Jeremiah. Still another bore the name of the scribe Azariah, son of Hilkiah while another belonged to Jerehmeel, the grandson of King Jehoiakim. These figures are named in the Chapter 22 of 2nd Kings and Chapter 36 of Jeremiah. Their fates are intertwined in the years prior to the Babylonian destruction. We are introduced to them during the 18th year of the heroic King Josiah, as they were renovating the Temple of Solomon,

> "Hilkiah the high priest said to Shaphan the secretary, 'I have found the Book of the Law in the temple of the LORD.' He gave it to Shaphan, who read it. Then Shaphan the secretary went to the king and reported to him: 'Your officials have paid out the money that was in the temple of the LORD and have entrusted it to the workers and supervisors at the temple.' Then Shaphan the secretary informed the king, 'Hilkiah the priest has given me a book.' And

Shaphan read from it in the presence of the king. When the king heard the words of the Book of the Law, he tore his robes. "[4]

What does the discovery of a Torah scroll in King Josiah's day have to do with our little seals?

Finding those little bits of clay with the names of Hilkiah and Shaphan shatters Higher Criticism as embraced by the likes of DeWette and Welhausen. This movement, which began in the early 1800's, in Germany, continues even today basically teaching that the Torah is simply a product of man's imagination. The main tenet of DeWette's theory is that Deuteronomy, the final book of the Torah, was written during reign of King Josiah. The brilliant Rabbi Marvin Antelman refutes DeWette's argument with salient Bible scholarship,

> "DeWette overlooks some basic facts that stare in the face of anyone who is intimately familiar with the manner and tenor of the Hebrew Bible. What is significant here is that the Biblical account tells that a manuscript of the Torah was *found* in Josiah's time by Chilkiyahu, the High Priest (2 Kings 22:3).[5] When the Bible tells us it was *found,* it is most significant that the Bible does not tell us that it was *written* by Chilkiyhau. Scripture tells us furthermore, that it was given to Shaphan the Scribe, for reading, who in turn brought it to the King. This narrative and this fact shed some very important light on the true function of the royal Priestly Scribe. The scribes were

> guardians of the Torah, and they knew it by heart in all its innuendos and preserved what is known as the authentic Massoretic text. It is significant that the Bible, on the spot tell us that Shaphan's grandfather was none other than Meshulam the Scribe. This information is vital and critical to a proper understanding of the narrative and tells us why Shaphan was competent to render judgment as to the authenticity of the found manuscript."[6]

Throughout the Bible, the importance of the priestly scribe is demonstrated continually.[7]

These *soferim* were simply carrying on the vital work of Moses whose own role as a scribe is dramatically evident as described in Deuteronomy 10:4. Where would the history of Israel be without the efforts of another famous priestly scribe known as Ezra?

Rabbi Antelman says the higher Biblical critics such as DeWette get a failing grade for their ignorance of the text and especially for their intellectual dishonesty,

> "...Because [DeWette's] thesis is based on assuming that Kings II is accurate. If he had taken the narrative of Chapter 22 of Kings II as authentic, then he would certainly have had to take Chapter 14 of Kings II as equally authentic. Chapter 14 records an incident which took place several generations before Josiah was born, where Amaziah, king of Judah, killed the people who deposed his father from the throne but did not kill their children because "as it is

written in the Torah of Moses, fathers should not be killed on account of their children, nor children on account of their fathers, but each shall perish on account of his own sins. (Kings II 14:6)."[8]

In the aforementioned verse, King Amaziah is quoting Deuteronomy 24:16. *However, the king is making reference to a law in a book that, according to DeWette's tortured logic, was not even written until nearly two hundred years later.* It would seem that the little clay seals recovered by archaeologist Yigal Shiloh confirm the genuine existence of Azariah and Gemariah and their sons, Hilkiah(the very same who found the Torah Scroll in Josiah's day) and Shaphan (the who witnessed the event).

The discovery of these bullae is an especially encouraging development. At the end of this book, I have devoted more pages (SEE APPENDIX A & B) to the impressive archaeological discoveries that connect events and figures of the Bible to tangible evidence unearthed from all over the Middle East.

Chapter Three Notes

[1] The essential differences are in the numbering of certain verses and the order of the books.

[2] Alan Millard, *How Reliable is Exodus,* Biblical Archaeology Review, pp. 51-57, July/August 2000

[3] ibid

[4] 2Kings 22:8

[5] This is a more accurate phonetic rendering of a Hebrew name usually anglicized as Hilkiah.

[6] Rabbi Marvin S. Antelman, *To Eliminate the Opiate*-Vol. I, p.147 (Zahavia Ltd. 1974)

[7] 1Kings 4:3, 2Kings 18:37, 2Samuel 8:5, Ezra 7:12

[8] Antelman, pp. 148-149

SECTION TWO
THE HEBREWS IN EGYPT

CHAPTER FOUR

The Hebrew Vizier

The actual story of the Exodus is common knowledge to anyone with even a passing interest in the Bible. For the reader who has never read the scriptural account, there might be some holes in the plot. So, let us briefly summarize the dramatic narrative, according to the Torah.

Chapter 37, in the book of Genesis, reveals how and why the family of Jacob first migrates to Egypt. It begins with a dream. Joseph, the son of Jacob, is sold

As Prime Minister of Egypt, Joseph commanded that the bounty of seven years be stored for the coming famine. His effectiveness as an administrator not only saved the nation, but was directly responsible for its growth into a world empire.

into slavery by his own brothers and later acquired by an Egyptian high priest. Joseph is wrongfully imprisoned. During his incarceration, the king of Egypt is troubled by a dream that he cannot understand. Joseph wins his release when the ruler is told that the young Hebrew prisoner can interpret dreams.

From Joseph, the troubled monarch learns that his dreams foretell seven years of plenty followed by seven years of famine. Joseph boldly outlines a detailed plan to save the country. Recognizing Joseph's wisdom, Pharaoh promotes him to Viceroy, second only to the King. Joseph gains the mantle of power at the age of 30. The young Hebrew soon distinguishes himself as an intelligent and skilled administrator. He organizes a national effort to store enough produce for the expected disaster.

The seven-year famine arrives and its effects are felt well beyond the borders of Egypt. Because the ravages of the famine are so severe, most Egyptian landowners sell their property to the crown. Joseph develops an ancient feudal system allowing the former landowners to stay on their property. As the nations come to Egypt for its abundant grains and bountiful produce, the country's economy is further enriched.

After two years of distress, the need for food brings Joseph's brothers to Egypt to buy grain. Joseph, realizing that his fate was all a part of God's plan forgives his brothers. They are reunited and the entire family immigrates to Egypt. The young Hebrew vizier sends word to his father Jacob,

> "...God has made me master of all Egypt. Come to me without delay." – Genesis 45:9

Jacob's household settles in *Goshen,* located in the rich Nile Delta region. There, the families or Twelve Tribes flourish. His talents as an administrator, an architect and military leader have a vital impact on the culture of Egypt. Through his leadership the country becomes a rich and powerful world empire that weathered the ravages of nature. Joseph rules as Viceroy for eighty years, dying at the age of 110.

Bondage

In the first chapter of the book of Exodus we are told that the Egyptians believed that the growing Hebrew population posed a threat to the nation's stability. Because of their endurance and their vast numbers Pharaoh's advisors were convinced that the Hebrews would eventually de-stabilize the nation, overthrowing the crown.

The Jewish Oral Tradition reveals that the Children of Israel were enticed to join the Egyptians in a massive public works project to fortify the borders and to expand the garrisons at Pithom and Rameses. The Hebrews enthusiastically joined in, motivated by patriotism that grew from their gratefulness to a country that had once welcomed them with open arms. It was the Egyptians who should have been grateful, but they eventually withdrew their own workers leaving only the Israelites. Soon, the Hebrew tribes were under guard in their own communities. The stone barriers that the Egyptians had convinced them to fortify over the years became prison walls.

> "The Egyptians appointed conscription officers over [the Israelites] to crush their spirits with

hard labor. [The Israelites] were to build up the cities of Pithom and Rameses as supply centers for Pharaoh." - Exodus 1:11-12

Rabbi Yaacov Culi in *Me'am Lo'ez* relates that the above verse uses the word *miskenoth* to describe this building project and points out that it is related to *sakanah*, a word denoting danger. The walls of these garrisons were so high that falling from one meant instant death.

If you really reflect on what was happening, the Egyptians had created the first concentration camps complete with *capos* who would spy on their own people.

At the time of their greatest suffering, God sent the Children of Israel a Deliverer. He was Moses, born of the priestly Tribe of Levi. It was his birth that prompted the Egyptians to implement an ancient form of eugenics to further thin the ranks of the Israelites. The Oral tradition relates that the astrologers of pharaoh discerned that a Hebrew child had been born who would destroy Egypt. These seers had also determined that the downfall of this hero would come by water. Thus, a decree was issued to throw the newborns into the Nile River. Probably under the guise of population control, thousands of infant Hebrew males were drowned.

"Pharaoh then gave orders to all his people: 'Every boy who is born must be cast into the Nile, but every girl shall be allowed to live.'" - Exodus 1:22

The Arks of Moses

There are two arks that figure in the life of Moses. The first is the little reed craft that carried him safely along the Nile into the arms of Pharaoh's daughter. The other is the Ark of the Covenant fashioned at Mount Sinai to house the Torah stones. There are two completely different Hebrew words employed for each of these boxes. The little reed vessel in Exodus 2:3 is called a *tevah* or *tevat*, the very same words used to describe the ark of Noah in Genesis 6:14. *Tevah* and *tevat* are never used for the Ark of the Covenant. This fabled golden box topped with winged *keruvim* is known as the *aron*. Keruvim and *aron* offer some interesting possibilities regarding the properties of the ark built at Sinai. The word *aron* comes from the root *ohr* which means "light". The root of the word *keruvim* is *karav* meaning to "draw near". The linkage of these two Hebrew words hints that the golden ark "gathers light or energy". In modern synagogues the Torah Scroll is held within an ark. Nowadays the Ethiopians claim that they have the Ark of the Covenant. In one of those curious meldings of language, legend and religion, the Ethiopian word for their Ark is *tabot*, a word that closely resembles *tevat*, the Hebrew word for the craft built by Noah. Interestingly, *aron* is also the word for coffin in the last verse of Genesis.

Fully aware that the astrologers did posses a limited grasp of prophecy, the parents of Moses hid their newborn son in a secure basket launching it into the Nile. Later, when the king's seers consulted the stars again, they would see that the child had surely been "thrown into the Nile" and ceased to search for him.[1]

Mirriam, the faithful older sister of Moses, watched from the banks as the little reed ark floated along the Nile.[2] The child is found by king's own daughter and raised in the palace, the very seat of power. As a young man, Moses witnesses an Egyptian overseer beating a Hebrew slave. He kills the overseer and flees for his own life. Years later, he finds his way to the house of Jethro, the High Priest of Midian. Moses eventually marries Zipporah, one of Jethro's daughters and settles down to a life domestic bliss. While watching the flocks of Jethro near Mount Sinai, God beckons to Moses, speaking from a burning bush. The Creator reveals to Moses his true destiny and also the reason that he must deliver Israel from bondage.

> "You must say to Pharaoh, 'This is what God says: Israel is My son, My firstborn. I have told you to let My son go and serve Me."
> – Exodus 4:22

At the age of eighty, Moses returns to face a new Pharaoh. He asks the ruler to allow the Israelites to go into the desert to worship God. The king refuses. A year of miraculous but frightening plagues follows. The tenth and final plague causes the death of every firstborn male whether man or beast. Finally, Pharaoh allows the slaves to go free. A weary, defeated Egyptian populace gives their gold, silver and their finest clothing to the departing Hebrews.

> "I will give you status among the Egyptians, and when you all finally leave, you will not go empty-handed. Every woman shall borrow articles of silver and gold, as well as clothing, from her neighbors or from the woman living with her. You shall load this on your sons and daughters, and you will thus drain Egypt [of its wealth]." - Exodus 3:21-22

Basically, the Israelites are paid their back wages for their years of bondage.

As they set out on their journey Pharaoh changes his mind and dispatches his army to stop the Israelites. God intervenes once again. When the advancing Egyptian army threatens to overtake them, the sea divides allowing the Hebrews to cross on dry land. The army follows the fleeing Hebrews through the parted sea. They are utterly destroyed when the massive walls of water come crashing down. Forty-five days after their departure from Goshen the Israelite tribes arrive at the foot of Mount Sinai. Five days later, Moses receives the Ten Commandments and Israel becomes the first nation in history to be established under the authority of the Creator of time and space.

Chapter Four Notes

[1] Apparently, the astrologers could read the signs but their interpretive powers were not fully developed. Moses would experience trouble via water but it would come much later in his life, at the Waters of Meribah.

[2] As with many Biblical figures, her name was a prophecy, combining the Hebrew words *marar*, meaning "bitterness" and *am* which means "people".

CHAPTER FIVE

Who Was the Pharaoh of the Exodus?

When did this pivotal event in the history of the Jewish people occur? If we can establish the proper time frame, possibly we can begin to unravel this riddle. The popular idea that the Exodus happened during the time of Rameses can be discarded for any number of reasons. First of all, there is nothing recorded during or after his reign that resembles the scope and the impact of the Exodus. The Biblical

It is highly unlikely that Ramases the Great was the Pharoah of the Exodus since testing on his mummy proves that he died from a dental infection and not drowning. (Relief of Ramases II from Karnak)

account makes it clear that the Ten Plagues that accompanied the Exodus sent the Egyptian empire into ruin. This is nowhere evident in the time of Rameses II.

> "Rameses reigned sixty-seven years, and at his death he left Egypt one of the largest and most powerful kingdoms on the earth..."

Detail of the Merneptah Stele showing the reference to Israel. The two human figures with three notches underneath is a determinative that denotes Israel as a distinctive people.

One the real prizes on display at the Cairo Museum is the so-called Israel Stele commissioned by 19th Dynasty Pharaoh *Merneptah.* It bears the oldest known extra-Biblical reference to ancient Israel. The stele is, for me, solid evidence that neither *Merneptah,* nor his father, Rameses the Great had anything to do with the Exodus. First of all, the mummified corpses of both pharaohs are with us today. Even if Pharaoh was swept away in the churning depths of the Reed Sea and his subjects had recovered the body, his remains tell a much different story.

In 1976, an international team of scientists was commissioned to halt the spread of a fungus that was literally eating away at the mummy of Rameses II. Radiation treatments eventually saved the rotting mummy. During their initial quest to determine the origin of the fungus the team employed a whole range of sophisticated methods that revealed new insights into the life and death of the long dead king. At the time of his demise, Rameses suffered from typical ailments associated with advanced age. He had a stooped posture, walked with a limp and suffered from abscesses in many of his teeth. In fact, the cause of death was blamed on general infection.[1]

Rameses II probably conducted one ancient Egypt's most aggressive publicity campaigns. His likeness survives, as this one at Luxor, in every part of Egypt.

But it is the very mention of Israel on this monument that argues against the direct involvement of Rameses or Merneptah in the Exodus experience. When the Twelve Tribes fled from Egypt they were simply know as Hebrews. The Creator ordained them as a kingdom of priests at Mount Sinai but the rest of the world did not recognize Israel as a geopolitical entity until the time of they had a king, well over four-hundred years after the Exodus.

Some historians have attempted to pass off a minor slave revolt as the kernel of a story that grew into a Hebrew myth. I believe the language of the Torah gives us a clue as to the proper time frame. At this point, it might be useful to tackle a curiosity of the text regarding the names of the pharaohs. Though the Egyptian monarchs influenced the lives of the Biblical patriarchs in significant ways, there is no name given for any of these rulers in the five books of the Torah. In the later books of the Bible we find many Egyptian monarchs named such as Shishak, Necho and Hophra.

The answer might be found in the Torah precept that forbids uttering the name of any idol.

> "Be careful to keep everything that I have said to you. Do not pronounce the name of another deity. You must not let it be heard from your mouth." - Exodus 23:13

This could include a person who is worshipped as a god. There is no doubt that during the Old Kingdom the pharaoh was considered godlike.

> "...he was from the first regarded as divine, although a little below the gods, but by the 5th Dynasty he came to be thought of as the actual

> son of the sun god. In the early years there was a tremendous chasm between him and his subjects which lessened in time for a variety of reasons."[2]

The Egyptians of the Old Kingdom were taught that their king was born of a virgin. The sun god, known as Ra, would impregnate the queen. Thus it was also taught that 'the blood of Ra flowed through the veins of every king.'[3] This cosmology was in place during the Egypt's so-called Early Dynastic and Old Kingdom periods. Since such a belief is an affront to the God of the Bible it could explain why the Torah refers only to title of Pharaoh while later Egyptian kings are specifically named in the later books of the Bible.

Prior to the Exodus, the Egyptian people actually believed that their pharaoh was a god. That blind devotion changed after witnessing pharaoh's downfall at the hands of the God of Moses. The utter destruction of their empire by God's hand surely must have put their ruler in a less flattering light. Egyptologist Cyril Aldred informs us that in the years following the decline of the Old Kingdom, in the dynasties known as the Middle Kingdom, the populace definitely viewed their monarch in more down to earth terms.

> "The prestige of the pharaoh as a divinity, already sadly eroded from the last years of the Old Kingdom, suffered further decay with the ascendancy of Osiris as the deification of the idea of kingship. From now on, all men who were worthy had the promise of immortality..."[4]

Aldred further comments that these Middle Kingdom rulers resorted to a kind of primitive public relations campaign to repair their tarnished image. They commissioned a series of fictional works such as *The Prophecy of Neferti, The Teaching of King Ammenemes* and the *Story of Sinuhe* that all portrayed the pharaohs as heroic characters.

> "These and some minor works, hymns in praise of the kings and so forth, form the classical literature of Egypt, and helped to enhance the prestige of the pharaoh during the Middle Kingdom."[5]

Prior to Exodus, the common people regarded the king divine. Historically, this was also the status of the pharaoh up until the end of the Old Kingdom. Even though subsequent Egyptian monarchs would continue to claim a godly ancestry, their subjects must have only acknowledged this conceit for political expediency. This drastic change in the way the Egyptian ruler was regarded, points to the Old Kingdom as the time of the Exodus.

"Let It Be Written...Let It Be So."

We can thank Cecille B. DeMille for reminding people that God gave the Torah to Israel but we can also charge him for propagating certain misconceptions that continue to color our understanding of this event. For his production, DeMille hired Henry Noerdlinger to research the script for the epic production. His exhaustive work led the scenarist to write the book, *Moses and Egypt* which was published shortly after the release of the feature film in 1956. It was Noerdlinger's belief that Rameses II was the Pharaoh of the Exodus.[6] This 19th Dynasty king was, like many tyrants, just a tad egomaniacal. The ancient public works devoted to keeping his memory alive must have been vast because the number of surviving monuments is still impressive. The name and image of Rameses the Great is found on everything in modern Egypt from hotels to military installations.

But there is nothing in his stony legacy that suggests anything like the Speilbergian events of the Exodus. If Rameses the Great was the Pharaoh of the Exodus where is it recorded during his reign?

Libraries and bookstores are stocked with countless editions that declare Rameses II as "Pharaoh of the Exodus". This misconception is either a misreading of the Biblical text but more often it is simply an educated guess. It is theory based wholly on the notion that a rich parcel of land located in the Nile Delta was named after the ruling pharaoh of that period—that Pharaoh being Rameses.

In the Bible, the name Rameses appears in exactly five places. Each time it is *only employed as a geographical reference.*[7] Turn to chapter 47 of Genesis and read how Joseph, the interpreter of dreams becomes vizier, a sort of prime minister of all Egypt. He also saved the country from famine and a grateful pharaoh invites Joseph's family to settle in the choicest region. In verse 6, pharaoh instructs Joseph,

"The land of Egypt is at your disposal. Settle your father and brothers in the best area. Let them settle in the Goshen district."

Reading down to verse 11 we learn that Goshen is known by another name.

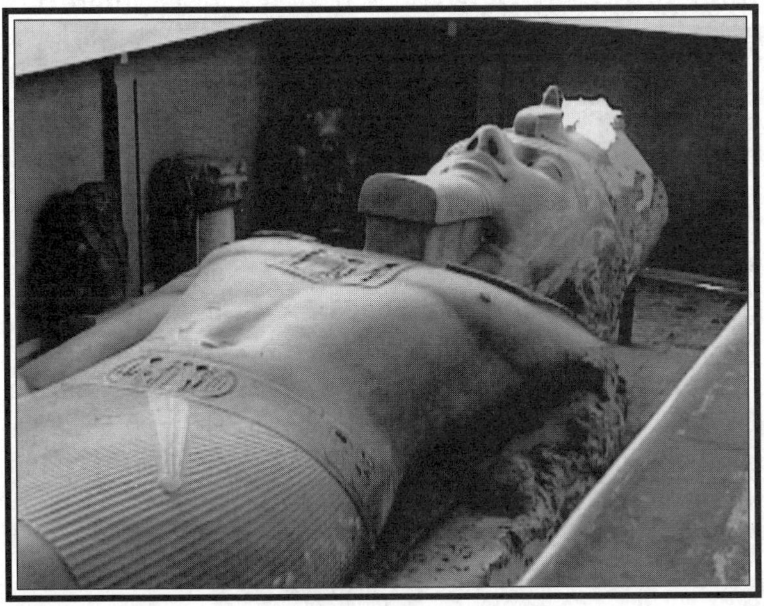

The fallen image of Rameses the Great on display in Memphis.

"Joseph found a place for his father and brothers to live. He gave them an estate in the Rameses region, in the best area, as Pharaoh had ordered."

It is obvious from the Biblical text that Goshen and Rameses are one and the same. Hundreds of years after Joseph invites the entire family to settle in Goshen we find their descendants enslaved while toiling away at two sites as described in Exodus 1:11 as Pithom and Rameses.

These two separate verses negate the theory that one of these cities was named for Rameses the Great. According to the existing Egyptian records, the name Rameses does not appear until the 19th Dynasty. The founder of that Dynasty, Rameses I only ruled two years. His son Seti ruled around eleven years and his son Rameses II (aka Rameses the Great) was king for sixty-five years.[8] These three kings ruled for a total of seventy-eight years.

The span of time from the first pharaoh Rameses and his grandson is less than eighty years. The duration between Joseph and the Exodus is far longer.[9] This imagined timeline is also problematic because Joseph was Prime Minister of Egypt for eighty years. Chapter 16 of Exodus makes it clear that after Joseph's death, the Hebrews flourished and grew in numbers and that "there arose a new king who did not know Joseph."

If the office of prime minister were bestowed on Joseph during the reign of Rameses I then he would still have been serving the crown when Rameses II took the throne. The Bible makes it very clear, in the above verse that Joseph had passed away long before the arrival of the ruler who would oppress and enslave the Israelites.

Chapter Five Notes

[1] Jean Vercoutter, The Search for Ancient Egypt (Harry N. Abrams, NY, 1992) p.188

[2] A. Rosalie David, *The Egyptian Kingdoms*, ( ) p.14

[3] Arthur Versluis, *The Egyptian Mysteries* (Arkana Paperbacks, New York, 1988) p.68

[4] Aldred, *The Egyptians* (Thames & Hudson, London, 1987) p.135

[5] ibid, pp.135-138

[6] Katherine Orrison, *Written in Stone* (Vestal Press 1999) p. 36

[7] See Gen.47:11, Ex.11:1,Ex.12:37, Num.33:3 and Num.33:5

[8] Sir Alan Gardiner, *Egypt of the Pharaohs*, p.445 (Oxford University Press 1961)

[9] The Midrash teaches only 210 years. However, that span still overshoots the combined rule of Rameses I, Seti and Rameses II.

CHAPTER SIX
The Upright Book

Let us consult an ancient Jewish source handed down for centuries entitled *Sefer Ha Yashar*. It is also known as the *Book of the Generations of Adam*. The first century Jewish sage known as Rabbi Eliezer, son of Hyrkanos quotes liberally from this nearly forgotten text. My personal library contains two versions of *Sefer Ha Yashar*, one published in 1993 and distributed by KTAV Publishers. The editor of the latter, Avraham Davis, maintains that though the origins of the work are uncertain, Jewish scholars have cited it for ages.

The first known printing was in Naples in 1553. *Sefer Ha Yashar* is also quoted throughout the exhaustive nineteen volume Torah anthology called *Me'Am Loez* written nearly 250 years ago by the great Sephardic sage Rabbi Yaakov Culi. The language of this text reflects a grasp of geography that is definitely post-Biblical with references to locales such as Lombardy and Tuscany.[1]

The first English translation of *Sefer Ha Yashar* was published in 1840 and is now available from Artisan Press in Muskogee, Oklahoma. The original translation contains numerous letters from Hebrew and Biblical scholars attesting to the authenticity of the work. Those commendations are missing from the newer editions but thanks to the tireless efforts of author Wayne Simpson, those endorsements have been reprinted in an edition called *The Authentic Annals of*

Sefer Ha Yashar is a work rich in plot and equally dense in detail. If screenwriters drew from the accounts as we find them in this Midrash, their scripts would burst with dramatic imagery. In the chapters devoted to birth of Moses we learn of a certain advisor to Pharaoh by the name of Reuel. When the Egyptian king decides that the Children of Israel might soon become a threat, Reuel reminds Pharaoh of all the good that the Hebrew Joseph had done for Egypt. Unhappy with this advice, the king turns to his other advisors, Balaam and Job. While Balaam tells Pharaoh to throw the Hebrew children into the Nile, Job takes a neutral position allowing that Pharaoh should do what he thinks is best.

Reuel realizes that he has fallen out of favor with the crown and decides to leave. He immigrates to the land of Midian where he becomes known as a High Priest called Yithro(Jethro).

Years later, when a full-grown Moses visits Yithro he discovers a sapphire rod planted in the great seer's garden. Moses is told that no man can pull this rod from the ground except the one who would deliver the Children of Israel from their bondage. Many had tried and failed but Moses plucks the rod from the earth. Engraved on the rod was the Tetragrammaton, the holy, unpronounceable name of God.

the Early Hebrews.[2] I recommend Simpson's edition, not only for its reader friendly format, but also for his own thought provoking commentaries in the book's appendix section.

The English title, *Book of Jasher,* often confuses those unfamiliar with Hebrew. Some construe *jasher* as the author's name. However, the word is a translation of *yashar,* meaning straight or upright. I have checked this latter version with many of the specific events mentioned in *Me'Am Loez* and found them to be consistent. Historians will immediately object to my turning to what they consider an obscure text. Even using the Bible and related sources for historical research is always considered problematic. I will be warned that I am on shaky ground relying on such "legendary" sources. They will question my drawing from material derived from religious sources. However, the very origins of Greece and Rome are handed down to us from Herodotus, Eusebius and Titus Livius. These authors of antiquity all had to depend on legendary material. It is a fact that many ancient cultures cannot decisively pinpoint their own beginnings. For instance, much of Rome's early history is really the province of poets like Virgil and Ennius. I have to agree with historian Will Durant who said,

> "We must not ignore these stories...they may contain more history than we suppose; and they are so bound up with Greek poetry, drama and art that we should be at a loss to understand these without them.[3]

No Term Limits in Antiquity

The harsh burdens inflicted on the Hebrews began with ascension to the throne of a king described in the book of Exodus as one "who knew not Joseph". In *Sefer Ha Yashar,* we learn that the name of this Pharaoh is ***Melol.*** Due to the severity of his decrees, the Hebrews called him ***Meror,*** a name taken from the root word for bitterness. He had commanded that all Hebrew male children should be thrown into the Nile. Pharaoh further decreed that if any slave failed to meet their daily quota of bricks, the overseers were to take the youngest child of the slave and use the infant in place of bricks and mortar. Melol is the known as the Pharaoh of the Oppression.[4]

What is most remarkable about this tyrannical king is the length of his reign.

> "Melol was twenty years old when he began to reign, and he reigned for ninety-four years."[5].

It was the daughter of this king who would later discover Moses in the river and raise him as a Prince of Egypt. During the last ten years of his life, Pharaoh Melol was smitten with severe skin disorders and intestinal problems. He believed that bathing in the blood of Hebrew infants would cure him.

When Melol finally died in agony, his body was in such a state of decay; no one wanted to approach it. His first-born, *Othri* should have succeeded him on the throne, but he was found to be mentally incompetent. His brother *Adikam* was selected to reign.

The Son Also Rises

"Adikam was twenty years old when he reigned over Egypt, he reigned four years."[6]

Sefer Ha Yashar also relates something unusual about the physical aspect of young Adikam. The populace nicknamed him *Ahuz,* their word for "short". He was said to stand only a cubit and a span in height. It is apparent that Melol was very old when he fathered Adikam. According to modern medical authorities, the chances of a child being born a dwarf can increase dramatically when the father is advanced in years.[7]

It was during the final twelve months of Adikam's reign that the Ten Plagues occurred, climaxed by the death of the firstborn. Remember, his older brother *Othri* was supposed to rule but was found to be incompetent. This would explain why Pharaoh Adikam did not perish during the death of the first-born. Adikam would survive that calamity but he would witness the might of his armed forces drowning in the Sea of Reeds.

Chapter Six Notes

[1] *Meam Loez* was translated by the brilliant late Aryeh Kaplan, of blessed memory.

[2] Available from Simpson at 629 Lexington Road, Sapulpa, OK, 74066 or his website at www.jasher.com

[3] Durant, *The Life of Greece* (Simon & Schuster, NY,1959) p.38

[4] It was earlier noted that sacred texts would not name someone like pharaoh since he was deified however; *Sefer Ha Yashar* is considered an historical work and not a sacred text.

[5] *The Book of Jasher* (Artisan Publishers, Muskogee, OK) p. 189

[6] ibid pp.218-219

[7] Bonnie M. Sampsell, *Ancient Egyptian Dwarfs*, KMT (Fall 2001,Vol. 12, Number 3) p.63

CHAPTER SEVEN

Searching the Egyptian Records

Every student of Egyptology knows Manetho's *History of Egypt,* but the original work does not exist today. Fragments of Manetho's work survive through four other ancient historians: Josephus, Africanus, Eusebius and Herodotus. However, they only quote fragments of the original. Manetho recorded the names of the ancient Pharaohs and the length of their reigns. Thanks to the years of extensive digging in Egypt, there is an abundance of ancient textual and archaeological sources to aid us in the search for the father and son who fit the description of the Pharaoh of the Oppression and the Pharaoh of the Exodus.

The entrance to the Temple of Seti at Abydos located along the Nile in Southern Egypt.

Abydos is known today as Abtu. Security logistics make it necessary to first journey south from Cairo to Luxor (about 8 hours by car) then drive back north under police escort the 90 miles to the temple site.

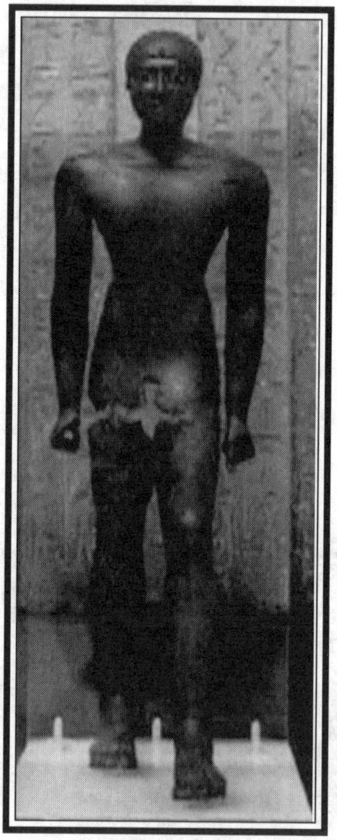

In the vast Cairo Museum, near the central hall, encased in glass is statue of keen interest. It is one of the oldest metal statues in the world. Fashioned in copper is the likeness of the Sixth Dynasty king Pepi. *The nearly life-sized statue was uncovered in 1897, about 400 miles south of Cairo by archaeologist James Quibell.*[3] *Found within it was a smaller figure believed to be his son* Pepi II.

Seti, the father of Rameses built the temple to carry on the worship of Osiris. It was first excavated in 1864. Near the rear of the temple, on a wall covered with *cartouches,* is the King's List of the early Pharaohs of Egypt. It is a record of seventy-five kings from the First

Dynasty up to the Nineteenth Dynasty. It was Rameses the Great who commissioned this ancient roll call to pay homage to his forerunners. This gallery bears the prenomen of Neferkare, also known as *Pepi II.*

Inscribed on the chamber's right side , in the Kings Gallery at Abydos, are the titles of almost every pharaoh from the first 19 dynasties of ancient Egypt.

The Turin Royal Canon is actually a papyrus discovered in 1822. The hieratic text also lists many of the pharaohs from the First to the Nineteenth Dynasties. It was also written during the time of Rameses the Great. Manetho's Dynastic list found some corroboration thanks to the Turin Royal Canon. An Italian tourist, Bernardino Drovetti, discovered it in 1822. This scroll derives its name from the museum in Turin, Italy where it remains on display.

Written in a cursive form of hieroglyphs called hieratic, the Papyrus also lists many of the Pharaohs

In the Kings Gallery at Abydos is the cartouche of Neferkare Phiops, aka Pepi II, who ruled Egypt for an incredible 94 years

and the length of each reign. In these ancient Egyptian catalogues we can discover a startling correlation between the Jewish and Egyptian records. These chronicles list a Sixth Dynasty ruler known as *Pepi II*. He was also called *Neferkare Phiops, Merenre and Nemtimsaf I*. This pharaoh is well known for having ruled longer than any king in all of Egyptian history, an astonishing **94 years**.[1]

This is an important detail about the king because it matches what the Jewish Midrash relates about *Melol*, the king who enslaved the Hebrews. He was the pharaoh "who knew not Joseph." *Melol* is called the Pharaoh of the Oppression and **he ruled 94 years**![2]

If we look at the listing of kings that comes to us from the Egyptian historian Manetho we find another possible connection to this family of Sixth Dynasty pharaohs. His name is *Othoes* which sounds very much like

Othri who should have succeeded his father on the throne but found to be mentally unstable. The son who would reign was *Adikam*. According to *Sefer Ha Yashar* he only ruled for four years. Looking again to the Egyptian records we find that the son of *Pepi II, Neferkare the Younger* succeeded him on the throne. He was known variously as *Merenre* and *Nemtimsaf II*. His reign was only a one year.

This limestone statue of Khnumhotep found at Sakkara is a faithful rendering of a young achondroplastic dwarf. Could this Sixth Dynasty figure also represent the likeness of Adikam Ahuz, the Pharaoh of the Exodus?

Here we have two fascinating parallels between two very different sources: The Egyptian chronicles carved in stone at Abydos and the ancient papyrus now housed in Turin both echo what we find in the Jewish Midrash. Why are the names of these rulers so dissimilar?

The confusion comes from the fact that the ancient kings of Egypt had as many as five names. Some are titles while other appellations are various forms of the birth name, expressed as the Prenomen and Nomen, the Nebty name, Horus name, and the Golden Falcon name. The ancient Egyptians were very superstitious in this regard. Since they were concerned with the afterlife, they wanted to insure that their name was not forgotten. Even if a carved likeness of the deceased was left behind it was of no use unless it bore their name.

> "Without a naming inscription either on the statue or nearby, a statue represented no one. Without a name an ancient Egyptian did not exist. The possibility of losing one's name and therefore one's existence was a very real fear, so much so that a prayer for remembrance was included in the Book of the Dead."[4]

It is therefore no surprise that the kings of antiquity had so many names. Apparently they suffered from a bit of insecurity. Five or more names will go a long way in the afterlife. The Old Kingdom rulers might possess other names that we have not yet learned. There is an interesting linguistic problem that may reveal another link between the name of Pharaoh *Pepi II* and *Melol*. The Egyptian tongue had difficulty with the "l" sound and the "r" sound. The hieroglyph could be articulated either way. Since *Pepi II* was also known as *Merer*, it might be translated as something akin to *Melel*, or as he was known to the Hebrews, *Melol*.

Whatever these two Sixth Dynasty kings were called, it is intriguing to consider that *Pepi II* may have been the Pharaoh of the Oppression who enslaved the Israelites and his son, *Neferkare the Younger,* the Pharaoh of the Exodus. This possibility leads us to another extraordinary parallel and that is the climactic downfall of the Old Kingdom.

Chapter Seven Notes

[1] Aldred, *The Egyptians* (Thames & Hudson, London 1984) p. 65

[2] *Odyssey Magazine* (March/April 200) p. 18

[3] Sefer Hayashar (KTAV Publishing, Hoboken, NJ, 1993)p.167

[4] Hilary Wilson, *Understanding Hieroglyphs*, (Michael O'Mara Books 1995) p.29

CHAPTER EIGHT
Twilight of the Old Kingdom

Egyptologists draw a demarcation line at the close of the Sixth Dynasty. They say it is the culmination of an epoch known as the Old Kingdom.

> "The Old Kingdom brought about the full appearance of Egyptian civilization on the world stage. We see it as a stable entity insured of longevity by its well-rooted traditions and well-balanced economy. The brilliance of achievements in engineering, in the creation of businesslike writing as an adjunct to hieroglyphs, the firm religious philosophy, the moral code, the technology which made use of raw materials, and above all the enormous agricultural productivity—made Egyptian culture increasingly dominant over all others in the vicinity and for a considerable distance beyond."[1]

The Egyptian empire was experiencing a golden age and that is what makes its fate all the more surprising. At the close of the Sixth Dynasty, sometime after the rule of a Pharaoh known variously as *Pepi II, Merenre* and *Neferkare,* Egypt exited the world stage. It fell as a world empire. On this point, most Egyptologists agree.

> "At this distance of time, the overthrow of the Old Kingdom at the end of the Sixth Dynasty has all the appearance of being sudden and complete"[2]

"Conflicting as these accounts may appear, they convey an impression of the same historic fact: the morrow of the passing of Pepy II witnessed a lapse into political anarchy."[3]

"After the death of Nefer-ka-ra, Egyptian history is involved in darkness and confusion."[4]

Statue of a scribe in the Cairo Museum. This figure, from the Old Kingdom period, exhibits a delicate life-like quality that was typical of the Old Kingdom and marked the era as a Golden Age.

All the sources point to a time of upheaval that marked the demise of the Old Kingdom. There was not even a standing army! The king's lists attest to this rapid decline with Manetho reporting that seventy kings ruled in seventy days.

"Anarchy, violence and poverty were followed by famine, plague and utter depression. The old people who had lived through the peace and security of the Old Kingdom must have suffered the most, but no one was safe from marauding thieves, hunger and fear. It was a topsy-turvy world."[5]

Oddly, these calamities allegedly resulted from the gradual erosion of the pharaoh's power base. Most Egyptologists can only surmise that the culture imploded and fell prey to the onslaught of aggression from beyond its borders. Since the debate is still open on this point, we can entertain another possibility. The answer is readily offered by the graphic depiction of the events that preceded the departure of the Israelites from Egypt.

Consider the fate of Egypt as recounted in the Biblical narrative:

■ The land and people suffer through twelve months of dreadful plagues that destroys crops, livestock and other resources.

■ Still reeling from those hardships the populace witnesses the death of every first- born male throughout the land of Egypt.

■ The Egyptians voluntarily hand over their fortunes in gold and silver to the Israelites.

■ The nation's total labor force, the Hebrew slaves departs and with them a mixed multitude.

■ Finally, with the drowning of the Egyptian military leadership in the Sea of Reeds, the country is rendered completely defenseless and the male population is further depleted.

What nation, even today, could survive such an unrelenting series of blows? I believe these factors, cited above, all contributed to the utter ruin of the empire, bringing the nation to its knees and plunging it into a dark age that continued for hundreds of years, as attested to in the Egyptian sources. This is echoed in the Biblical record. Not until the time of Solomon do we encounter the Egyptians as a world power again—over four hundred years after the Exodus.[6]

There is no denying that the end of the Sixth Dynasty and the Old Kingdom saw Egypt plunged into a time of chaos. Some of the previously quoted sources give the impression that it came during the reign of *Pepi II*. However, the final chapters of that epoch actually played out during the rule of his son, *Neferkare the Younger*, or as he is also known, *Nemtimsaf*.

Queen for a Day?

On the southwest corner of the Giza plateau is another possible connection to the Exodus. It is known as the Pyramid of *Mykenirus*. This is the so-called Third Pyramid. It supposedly belongs to a Fourth Dynasty king. The historian Manetho claims that "the third pyramid was built by Nitocris."[7] This seeming discrepancy could be explained by the fact that the monument was first built by *Mykenrius* and later enlarged by *Nitocris*. The pyramid contains two burial chambers. The remains of *Mykenirus* rested within a wooden coffin in the lower vault while the upper contained a blue basalt sarcophagus. It is possible that this stone crypt was the final resting place of *Nitocris*.[8]

4th Dynasty Pharaoh Mycerinus flanked by the goddess Hathor and the god of Diospolis. Did Queen Nitocris refurbish his pyramid for her own use?

Nitocris is also known by her prenomen *Menkaura* which sounds very close to *Mykenrius*. Manetho further claims that *Nitocris* was the last ruler of the Sixth Dynasty. Her name was a Greek corruption of *Netiquerti* which is how she is listed on the ancient canon called the Turin Papyrus. She may have been the first woman pharaoh in the history of Egypt.

Egyptologist Barbara Mertz believes that the sudden appearance of a female on the throne was notable.

> "The ultimate ruler of the (6th) dynasty was a woman; any man, including Manetho, could tell you that this was a bad sign. If it were not for a reference to this lady, whose name was Nitocris, in the Turin Papyrus, I would be inclined to suspect her of being apocryphal as are the stories the Greeks collected about her."[9]

Until the reign of *Nitocris* the scepter of power had passed to the male heir...after all, the pharaoh was known as the Son of the Sun. If we factor in the Torah account of the death of the first born along with the drowning of the Egyptian army there would be a serious lack of male heirs for the throne of Egypt. The Torah and Midrash make it very clear that the Pharaoh of the Exodus did not return from the Sea of Reeds. Is it not conceivable that *Nitocris* reigned in his stead?

Since her ascension to the throne coincides with the disastrous final days of the Sixth Dynasty we can add this occurrence as another intriguing parallel to our Exodus account. If *Pepi II* and *Neferkare* the Younger, are respectively *Melol,* the Pharaoh of the Oppression and *Adikam,* the Pharaoh of the Exodus, then we should be able to find documents from the end of the Old Kingdom era that describe the shattering events of the Exodus Plagues.

Notes on Chapter Eight

[1] Fairservis, *The Ancient Kingdoms of the Nile* (Thomas Y. Crowell, NY, 1962) p. 81

[2] Cyril Aldred, *The Egyptians*, (Thames & Hudson 1984) p.120

[3] Donald B. Redford, *Egypt, Canaan and Israel in Ancient Times*, (Princeton University Press 1992) p.59

[4] Heinrich Brugsch-Bey, *Egypt Under the Pharaohs*, (Bracken Books 1902) p.50

[5] A. Rosalie David, *The Egyptian Kingdoms*, (Elsevier Phaidon, New York, 1975) p. 16

[6] Solomon makes a pact with pharaoh in 1Kings 3:1 but prior to Solomon, King Saul debriefs an Egyptian slave who has escaped from the army of Amalek. In Saul's day, Amalek occupied the Eastern border of Egypt near present day El Arish.

[7] Barbara Mertz, Temples, Tombs and Hieroglyphs (Peter Bedrick Books, NY, 1990) p.97

[8] Heinrich Brugsch-Bey, *Egypt Under the Pharaohs* (Bracken Books, London) p.50

[9] Mertz, *Temples, Tombs & Hieroglyphs* (Peter Bedrick Books 1990) p.97

SECTION THREE
LEAVING EGYPT

CHAPTER NINE

The Amazing Papyrus at Leiden

"The sound of Your thunder was in the whirlwind: the lightnings lightened the world: the earth trembled and shook. Your way is in the sea, and Your path in the great waters, and Your footsteps are not known. You led your people like a flock by the hand of Moses and Aaron."
-- Psalms 77:18

Once the seat of Old Kingdom power and splendor, much of the ruins of Memphis (Menifir) still await excavation.

God sent Ten Plagues against the nation of Egypt, each more devastating than the last. The Egyptians would endure these calamities for twelve months. It is an epic marked by howling storms, seismic events and possibly volcanic activity. Elsewhere in the Bible we can find descriptions of the disasters that accompanied the Ten Plagues. If we look more closely at the Biblical account of the Exodus we see a time of massive upheavals in the natural order of the world. Surely the Ten Plagues and the attendant chaos would have been memorialized in some fashion? We may just have such a record.

Housed in the Museum of Leiden in the Netherlands is a crumbling papyrus first unearthed near the pyramids at Saqqara in 1822. The museum purchased them in 1828 from a private collector named Anastasi. The text, a lengthy diatribe against the king by a priest named Ippuwer, was translated into English in 1909 by Egyptologist Sir Alan Gardiner and published as *The Admonitions of an Egyptian Sage.* Gardiner in his *Egypt of the Pharaohs* was adamant regarding the nature of the text,

> "This extremely tattered papyrus in the Leyden collection dates from no earlier than Dynasty XIX, but the condition of the country which it discloses is one which cannot be ascribed to the imagination of a romancer, nor does it fit into any place of Egyptian history except that following the end of the Old Kingdom."[1]

While other translators believed that the discourse of Ippuwer was prophetic in nature, Gardiner demonstrates, in his introductory remarks to his own translation, that the descriptive passages were far too detailed to be taken as predictions. "There is a limit to the minuteness with which future things may be foretold."[2]

Gardiner further dispels this notion by noting that the terrible state of things is familiar to those Ippuwer is addressing—that the miseries were foretold by the ancestors. That the sage was speaking of his present condition is further underscored by his pleas to take some kind of action. Another interesting aspect of this document is the fact that Ippuwer places the blame for his nation's ills squarely on the shoulders of the pharaoh.[3] The King's advisors do the same in the Bible.

> "Pharaoh's officials said to him, "How long will this man be a snare to us? Let the people go, so that they may worship the Lord their God. Do you not yet realize that Egypt is ruined?"
> -- Exodus 10:7

The papyrus, written in the cursive form called hieratic is an exhaustive litany of woes. Here, Ippuwer, addresses the court and mourns for the fallen state of his nation and people:

> "Mirth has perished and is no longer. There is groaning throughout the land mingled with lamentations...the land is in darkness"

> "Forsooth, the land turns round as does a potter's wheel...Upper Egypt is waste...All is

ruined...Oh that the earth would cease from its noise."

The most striking characteristic of this record is how the text details a chain of calamities that are strikingly similar to events found in the Biblical plagues.

Let's compare some of the Biblical descriptions with the language of the Ippuwer Papyrus:

Water to blood

In Exodus 4:9, God instructs Moses,
"...you shall take some water from the Nile and spill it on the ground. The water that you will take from the Nile will turn to blood on the ground."

Papyrus 7:4
"Behold Egypt is poured out like water. He who poured water on the ground, he has captured the strong man in misery.

Papyrus 2:6
Plague is throughout the land. Blood is everywhere.

Papyrus 2:10
"Forsooth, the river is blood."

Plague of Hail

Compare still more frightening events in Exodus with the words of Ippuwer,

> "Moses pointed his staff at the sky, and God caused it to thunder and hail, with lightning striking the ground. God then made it hail on the land of Egypt. There was hail, with lightning flashing among the hailstones." - Exodus 9:23-24

> Papyrus 2:10
> "Forsooth, Gates, columns and walls are consumed by fire."

Plague of Insects

> "The locust covered the entire surface of the ground, making the ground black. They ate all the plants on the ground and all the fruits on the trees, whatever had been spared by the hail. Nothing green remained on the trees and plants throughout Egypt." - Exodus 10:15

> Papyrus 6:2-4
> "Forsooth...no fruits or herbs are found...Forsooth grain has perished on every side."

Plague of Darkness

"Moses lifted his hand toward the sky, and there was an opaque darkness in all Egypt, lasting for three days"-Exodus 10:22

Papyrus 9:8-10
"Destruction...the land is in darkness"

Death of First Born

The most devastating blow of all was the death of the first born which occurred at midnight as we read in Exodus 12:29:

"It was midnight. God killed every first-born in Egypt, from the first-born of Pharaoh, sitting on his throne, to the first-born of the prisoner in the dungeon, as well as every first-born animal."

Sefer Ha Yashar tells that this punishment even extended to their stone images of the first-born and even the buried remains of the recently departed first-born of the Egyptians.[4]

Now, note the vivid similarity in the descriptions found in the Ippuwer Papyrus:

Papyrus 2:13
"Forsooth, men are few. He who places his brother in the ground is everywhere".

Papyrus 4:3
"Children of Princes are dashed against walls. The offspring of nobility are laid out on the high ground."

Papyrus 7:4
"The residence is overturned in a minute."

Spoiling Egypt

Finally, before their departure from Egypt, the Israelites are told to take the gold and silver from the Egyptians...sort of back wages for their years of unpaid labor.

> "The Israelites did as Moses had said. They requested gold and silver articles and clothing from the Egyptians. God made the Egyptians respect the people, and they granted their request. [The Israelites]drained Egypt of its wealth
> -- Exodus 12:35

Ippuwer again documents a parallel to this event.

Papyrus 2:4
"Forsooth, poor men have become the owners of good things. He who could not make his own sandals is now the possessor of riches."

Papyrus 3:3
"Gold, blue stone, silver, malachite, carnelian, bronze and Yebet stone and ....are fastened to the necks of female slaves."

Papyrus 8:2

"Behold the poor of the land have become rich, and [the possessor] of property has become one who has nothing.

The Mixed Multitude

As the Israelites took leave of Egypt they were joined by a "mixed multitude" as described in Exodus 12:38,

> "And a mixed multitude went up also with them; and flocks, and herds, even very much cattle."

The *erev rav* or mixed multitude comprised the Egyptian families who cast their fate with the Israelite tribes and departed with them. Though Gardiner found this next line from Ippuwer "hopelessly obscure", it makes perfect senses when compared to the above passage from Exodus 12:38.

Papyrus 3:14

"Those who were Egyptians have become foreigners."

Pillar of Fire

Now compare the description of Israel's flight from the land and the miraculous clouds that accompanied them with another line from Ippuwer,

> "God went before them by day with a pillar of cloud, to guide them along the way. By night it appeared as a pillar of fire, providing them with light." -Exodus 13:21

> Papyrus 7:1
> *"Behold the fire mounted up on high. Its burning goes forth before the enemies of the land."*

These are but a few of the countless verses found in Lieden papyrus which capture the wonder, terror and misery of Egypt in the wake of the Ten Plagues and the departure of the Israelites.

> Papyrus 4:2
> "Noise is not lacking in span...There is no end to the noise."

> Papyrus 6:1
> "O that the earth would cease from noise, and tumult be no more!"

And finally, could the following line describe the loss of the pharaoh who failed to return from his pursuit of the departing Hebrew slaves at the Sea of Reeds?

Papyrus 7:2
"Behold things are done, that have never happened for long time past: **the king has been taken away by poor men."**

Notes on Chapter Nine

[1] Gardiner, *Egypt of the Pharaohs*, (Oxford University Press 1961) p.109

[2] Gardiner, *The Admonitions of an Egyptian Sage*, (Georg Olms Verlag 1990) p.7

[3] ibid, p.8

[4] Book of Jasher (Artisan Press, Muskogee, Oklahoma) p. 228

CHAPTER TEN

Splitting the Sea

Though the Bible offers a compelling account of Israel's departure from the crumbling Egyptian empire, scholars cannot agree on the actual route taken by the Twelve Tribes. Within this debate is the question of just where the miracle of the Reed Sea crossing occurred. By consulting both the Torah and the Midrash we can reasonably retrace the path. Remarkably, with the help of modern science it is also possible to mark the site where Israel crossed through the sea and witnessed the

According to the original Hebrew of the Bible, Israel passed through the waters of Yam Suf, *the Sea of Reeds. Some speculate that the crossing could have taken place near modern Lake Timsah.*

drowning deaths of the advancing Egyptian hordes. Before introducing you to the scientific aspect of this event, let us consider what the text reveals. Beginning with Chapter 13 in the book of Exodus we find several geographical hints.

"When Pharaoh let the people leave, God did not lead them along the Philistine Highway, **although it was the shorter route**. God's consideration was that if people encountered armed resistance, they would lose heart and return to Egypt."- Exodus 13:17-18

The Direct Route

Taking the "Philistine Highway" located due east of the Nile Delta would give them speedy access to their destination. (see map on page 107) They are commanded not to travel this ancient corridor running along the Mediterranean Coast because the Israelites might turn back, fearing war. The Hebrew rendering is *re-eh milchamah,* literally "see war." *Sefer Ha Yashar* sheds even more light on what could evoke such alarm.

Thirty years prior to the Exodus, a large contingent from the Tribe of Ephraim decided that the time of their redemption had arrived. They remembered that God had told their ancestor Abraham that his descendants, after being enslaved, would be set free.[1] They knew from this promise that four hundred years would elapse before the prophecy would be fulfilled. They erred by counting the four hundred year exile from the event described in Genesis 15:13 when Abraham was seventy years old. However, the prophetical clock would not start ticking until the birth of Isaac, thirty years later. The departure of the men of Ephraim, coming too soon, would literally have grave consequences.

Sefer Ha Yashar goes on to relate that these men of Ephraim took no provisions thinking they would buy what they needed from the locals living along the road. The route was the Philistine Highway, surely the quickest, straightest path to Canaan. Their journey did not go as planned because the villagers along the way refused to sell food to the men of Ephraim. Fighting broke out and the locals called on the nearby Philistines for aid. In the battle that followed, thousands of men of the Tribe of Ephraim were slaughtered. The brutal Philistines piled the dead into one massive forbidding heap. This grim memorial was still there, thirty years later when the Exodus began and would have surely struck terror into the hearts of the departing Israelites. This is another reason that the people did not travel the shortest route to their destination, east along the shores of the Mediterranean.

Heading due north would take them straight into the Mediterranean. Obviously, traveling west would lead them away from their destination. They would have to travel on a southerly course. However, there was another hazard with journeying too far south. It would lead them into the thick of populated Egypt.

The Direct Route Was Close To Goshen

This little detail reveals a very basic truth about the location of Goshen, home of the Hebrews during their exile in Egypt. If the Philistine Highway was close at hand, as the Biblical text relates, then the Land of Goshen must have been due west of this ancient thoroughfare. Sir Flinders Petrie, long considered the Father of Egyptology, believed that Rameses and Pithom, the store cities built by the Hebrew slaves, were Tel Rotab and Tel al Muskhuta, west of the modern town of Ismailia, on the Suez Canal. Just 20 miles northeast of Tel al Muskhuta (Pithom) is Al Qantara. This was the beginning of the old caravan route to ancient Syria and known to us as the Philistine Highway.

God Led Israel Down to the Sea

Another key element in this narrative is the amount of time that elapsed from Israel's departure until their arrival at the Sea. The Torah gives a specific date for the beginning of their journey.

> "[The Israelites] left Ra'meses on the 15th of the first month. " - Numbers 33:3

They trekked to Sukkoth and from there they moved onto to Etham, "at the edge of the wilderness." Israel was commanded to travel from Etham to Pi Hahiroth. The name of the latter site can be translated variously as "the mouth of freedom" or "Freedom Valley."

The *Sefer Ha Yashar* states that, on the following day, a contingent of Egyptian nobles was dispatched to this new campsite. The Egyptians were anxious to know when the Hebrews would return from their worship.

"Now, therefore this makes **five days** since you went, why do you not return to your masters?"
- *Sefer Ha Yashar* 81:14

Of course, Moses made it clear that they would not return to their former situation. The Egyptian squad nformed Pharaoh of Moses' refusal. Encouraged by Israel's position as sitting ducks, the king mounted an assault on Israel. The Egyptian chariot fleet arrived at Pi Hahiroth on the 6th day of Passover.[2] The frightened camp looks back to see the Egyptian horde. We learn from Exodus 14:19 that the Pillar of Cloud moves to their rear, shielding the Israelite camp from the Egyptians all night long.

Now, the Biblical narrative takes on an epic flavor as the Creator harnesses the forces of nature with awful and wonderful results.

"Moses extended his hand over the sea. During the entire night, God drove back the sea with a powerful east wind, transforming the seabed into dry land. The waters were divided. The Israelites entered the seabed on dry land. The water was on their right and left like [two] walls."
-- Exodus 14:21

Classical Jewish Bible commentators such as the Rambam and Ralbag both teach that one of the reasons that God sent a strong east wind was so that the Egyptians would believe that they were simply witnessing a natural occurrence. They further comment that the Creator always minimizes miracles and alters the laws of nature only when it is of the great consequence.[3] If this event can fall into the realm of understandable phenomena, how could we explain it?

A Little Help from Our Friends

Dr. Frank J. Little, Jr. is an Ecologist and Oceanographer who is, according to one his peers, "an immensely talented scientist."[4] It was Dr. Little who introduced me to something known as "wind set-down," which can only occur when specific geophysical and meteorological elements are in place. This rare oceanographic phenomenon results in literally the parting of waters, creating a path on dry ground. It also creates an accompanying hazard called a seiche wave that allows those same waters to return with rapid, dangerous force sweeping away anything or anyone its path. Dr. Little bases his unique view on the earlier work of Swedish oceanographer Bo Hellstrom. As Little states in his research,

"Our purpose is to return Hellstrom's Exodus hypothesis to the scientific community, plus quantify and update it in light of newly synthesized evidence."[5]

Hellstrom first published a Swedish language paper on the subject in 1924 entitled *"Israels Tag Genom Roda Havet"* which was translated into an English version in 1950 as "The Israelites' Crossing of the Red Sea". Since this paper is quite rare today, Dr. Little was kind enough to supply me with copies of both reports. The nearly forgotten Hellstrom was a pioneer in his field who studied the effects of wind moving across the water. His interest regarding the Biblical splitting of the sea came after his frequent visits to Egypt and Saudi Arabia. Hellstrom also searched the ancient accounts of historians Herodotus, Diodorus, Pliny and Strabo. Hellstrom notes that most coastal people are familiar with the fact that wind can affect the level of water. Though it is rare, he also cites several historical incidents where wind set-down was responsible for creating a path through *an inland body* of water. Here he quotes an historian, Picot, from his history of Geneva, Switzerland.

> "On the ninth of January, 1495 such a strong wind was blowing that the waters of the Rhone were forced as much as a quarter of a mile into the lake, and *it looked as though it was a mountain of water, which maintained itself for a whole hour.*" (emphasis added)

> "On the second of January, 1645, between seven and ten o'clock in the morning, after a storm had been raging all night, a hurricane arose which was so violent that, in places, the waters of the Rhone were again driven into the lake, so that for an hour, several persons went dry shod right up to the chains which enclosed the harbour, while others walked across an arm of the Rhone which divides la Monnaie from l'Ile."[6]

It should be noted that both of these events took place in the wintertime when the lake level is lower than usual. A relatively shallow body of water is one of the fundamentals necessary for wind set-down to occur. For Professor Hellstrom, the Lake Geneva accounts are a model for the miracle at the Sea of Reeds. More importantly, as Dr. Little points out, the northern end of what we now call the Red Sea is a perfect candidate for wind set-down. Such a long shallow body of water is prone to exaggerated wind-driven level changes.

Hellstrom learned that prior to the construction of the Suez Canal, the western arm of the Red Sea reached farther north up to the present day Lake Timsah, near the town of Ismailia. The building of the dam eventually drained this section of the gulf creating the Great Bitter Lakes and exposing the strip of land between the Great Bitter Lakes and Lake Timsah. This was supported by a study of the region's geology by Theodor Fuchs who found that Lake Timsah consisted of recent marine deposits from the Red Sea.[7]

Since the geologic record proves that modern-day Lake Timsah was the northern shore of the ancient sea why didn't the Israelites travel around it? According to chapter 14, God led the departing Hebrews back towards the sea. Apparently this was a diversionary tactic.

> "God spoke to Moses, saying, 'Speak to the Israelites and tell them to turn back and camp before Freedom Valley, between Tower and the sea, facing Lord of the North. Camp opposite it, near the sea. Pharaoh will then say that the Israelites are lost in the area and trapped in the desert." - Exodus 14:1-2

The Hebrew word used for "turn" is *shuv,* which is literally "to return." The above verse employs the word *bukh* meaning "confusion". Instead of traveling around the northern shore of the sea, the Hebrews were led south to camp beside a place called *Pi Hahiroth.* Israel seemed to be caught between Migdol ("tower"),

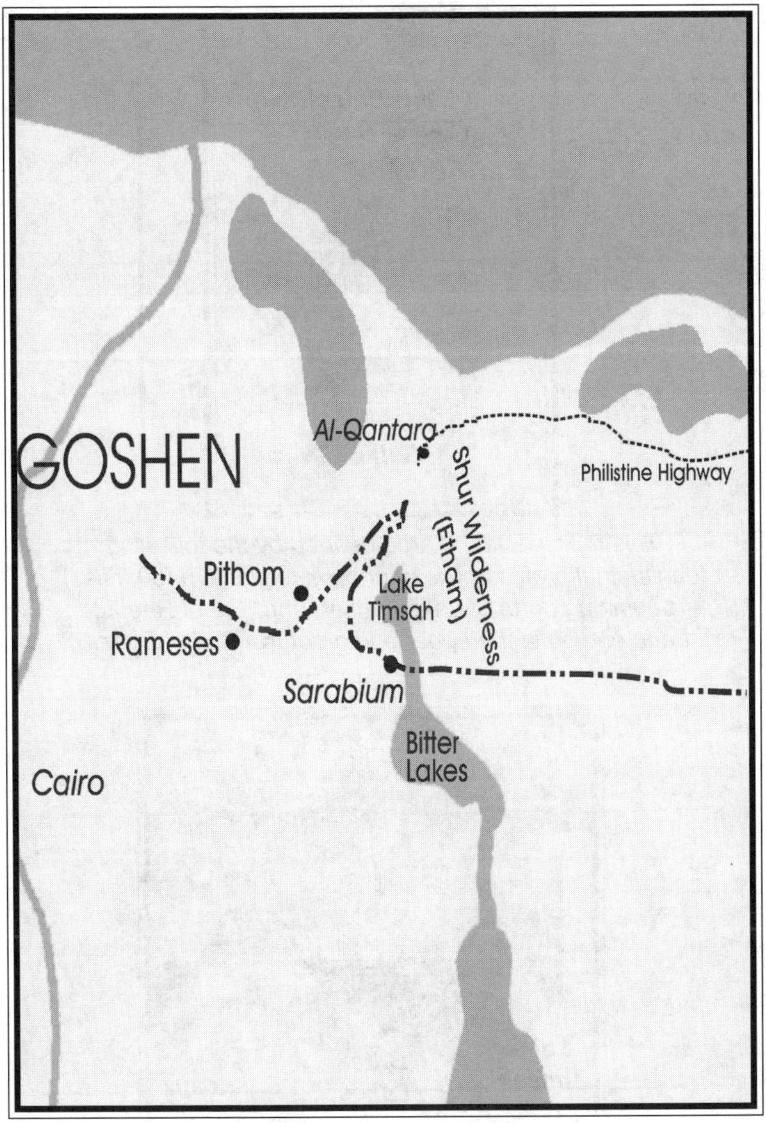
Al-Qantara
GOSHEN
Shur Wilderness
(Etham)
Philistine Highway
Pithom
Lake
Timsah
Rameses
Sarabium
Bitter
Lakes
Cairo

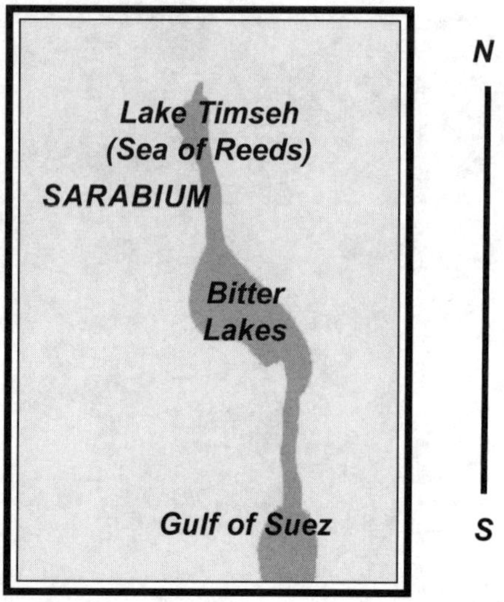

This represents the area defined by the following longitudinal profiles. It is approximately 90km (50 miles) beginning north of Lake Timsah (the Sea of Reeds) and ending in the upper portion of the Gulf of Suez.

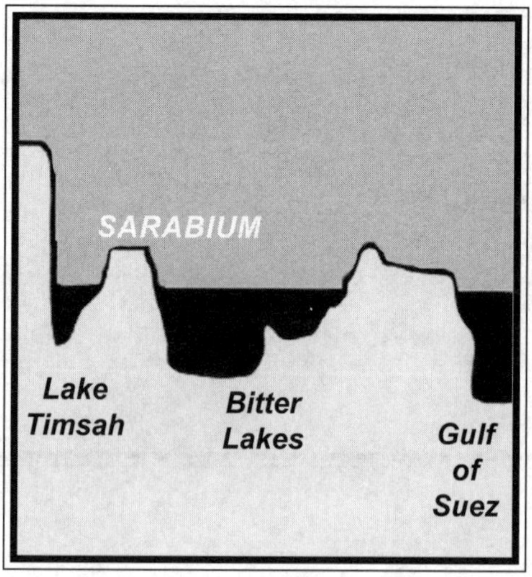

This is the present day water levels after the building of the Suez Canal.

This is the water level during the time of the Exodus, with no wind blowing.

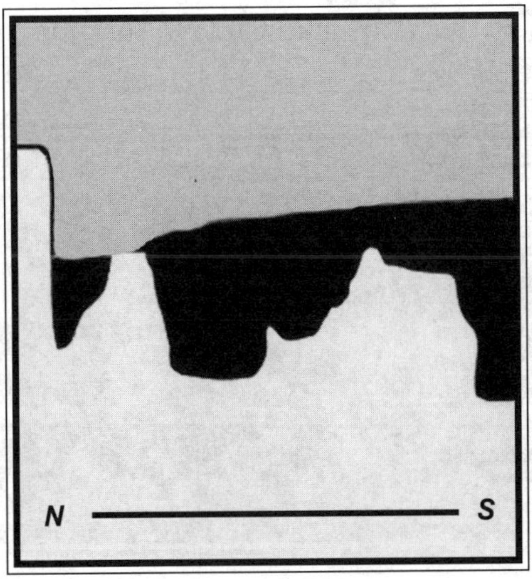

With the wind blowing from the North, the water would expose the land bridge south of Lake Timsah.

Baalzephon ("Lord of the North")[8] and the Sea. The late Rabbi Aryeh Kaplan describes the place where the Hebrews camped as a large plain, in a valley, between two massive pillars of stone that blocked their way out.[9] This scheme would ensure that Pharaoh would receive reports that the slaves appeared to have gotten lost and boxed in by these formations.

According to Professors Little and Hellstrom the actual locale, once under water is now dry ground. It is a five-mile wide strip of land that runs approximately one mile from west to east at present day *Serapeum* (*Sarabium*) on the banks of the Suez Canal. This site is perfect because the massive weather front could have blown in from the east (from Israel!) and collided with the prevailing northerly winds. These winds would have lowered the level of the sea, exposing the land bridge and piling the water up in the same manner as witnessed twice in Lake Geneva in later centuries.

Before the Suez Canal was constructed, the Gulf of Suez extended deeper inland encompassing Lake Timsah.

Some might object to what appears to be a minimizing of the miracle at the Sea of Reeds, by speculating that it occurred at the sight of a natural underwater bridge. But we must remember that if the splitting of the sea had taken place in extremely deep water, the Israelites could have very likely been faced with descending into an exposed shoreline that dropped off sharply. This could make for a difficult descent onto the dry sea floor and even harder ascent on the opposite exposed shoreline. For me, the real miracle is in the timing of these events. God had to reveal to Moses exactly when and where the sea would be divided.

The Bible, along with the Oral Tradition, tells us that the waters of the sea were like walls. There is a hint in this tradition that the east wind actually froze the waters on each side of the divide. The freezing is implied in the victorious Song of the Sea in Exodus 15:8 that states *kaf'u tehomot*, the "depths became dense". The phrase can also be rendered as "congealed" or "frozen." This and the aforementioned Plague of Darkness is consistent with the descriptions of the raging gales and unusual atmospheric phenomen recorded in the Bible as well as the Ippuwer Papyrus. The Jewish historian Josephus, in his Antiquities of the Jews, adds his own description of violent torrential conditions that accompanied the drowning of the Egyptians in the Sea of Reeds.

> "Showers of rain also came down from the sky and dreadful thunders and lightning, with flashes of fire. Thunderbolts also were darted upon them; nor was there anything which used to be sent by God upon men as indications of his

wrath which did not happen to them a this time, for a dark and dismal night oppressed them."[10]

Other ancient chronicles attest to a period of chaotic weather conditions. Herodotus writes of a legendary battle in the skies between Zeus and Typhon that ended in Egypt. Pliny the Elder speaks of a terrible comet seen from Egypt to Ethiopia. The comet was called Typhon. (This may be the origin of the raging storm at sea called a typhoon). Hevelius states that the very year that Israel departed from Egypt, a comet was seen in Syria, Babylon and India.[11]

By consulting the records of Herodotus, Diodorus, Pliny and Strabo, Hellstrom concluded that this natural land bridge at Serapeum was under the waters of the Red Sea from 1300 BCE to 1200 BCE, a time frame wholly consistent with that of Jewish Chronology which places Exodus at 1312 BCE.

Notes on Chapter Ten

[1] Genesis 15:13 details the promise given to the Patriarch while he is still called Abram.

[2] *Me'am Lo'ez* Volume 5 (Moznaim Publishers, NY & Jerusalem, 1979) p.179

[3] ibid, pp.195-196

[4] Dr. Phillip C. Hewitt, Emeritus and former Chairman of the Geology/Earth Scienes Department at SUNY-Brockport, New York

[5] Dr. Little, *Moses Parting of the Red Sea: The Meeting of Exodus, Geology and Oceanography* (Ecological Analytical Associates, Pittsford New York)

[6] Hellstrom, *The Israelite's Crossing of the Red Sea*, (English, Inst. Of Hydraulics, Royal Institute of Technology, Stockhom, 1950)p.20

[7] Hellstrom, *The Israelite's Crossing of the Red Sea*, (English version, Inst. Of Hydraulics, Royal Institute of Technology, Stockhom, 1950)p.13

[8] Baalzephon may have been a massive natural rock formation resembling an animal worshipped by the Egyptians

[9] Kaplan, *The Torah Anthology* (Moznaim Publishers, NYC, Jerusalem, 1979) p.161

[10] *The Complete Works of Josephus* (Kregel Publications, Grand Rapids, MI, 1981) p.64

[11] Immanuel Velikovsky, *Worlds in Collision* (Dell Books, N.Y, 5th Ed., 1969) p.96

CHAPTER ELEVEN
Monument to a Miracle

Journey about seventy miles northeast from Cairo and you will arrive at the little town of Ismailia, near the Suez Canal. If inquire about the local color you might be directed to a small museum that holds a tidy collection of antiquities. Housed in the main hall is a curious relic made of black granite and covered with hieroglyphs. It is a *naos* or shrine first discovered near El Arish in the 1860's.

A black granite naos or shrine discovered at El Arish in the 1860's. It gives the account of Pharaoh Thoum and his army pursuing their enemies only to perish at the "Place of the Whirlpool."

In 1890, F.L. Griffith published a translation of the text on the stone. It can be found in the pages of a book bearing the exhaustive title *The Antiquities of Tell el Yahudiyeh and Miscellaneous Work in Lower Egypt During the Years 1887-1888*. This artifact gives a most extraordinary account of the land of Egypt in the grip of nature gone rampant.

Hieroglyphs cover all four sides of the black granite naos on display in the archaeological museum in Ismailia

Photo by Gerald Payton

"Evil fell on the earth…the earth in great affliction...great disturbance in the residence..."

The narrative speaks of a tempest so dark and thick with debris that,

"…neither man nor the gods could see the faces of those next to them…"

The Fate of Pharaoh

Most rabbinical scholars assume that Pharaoh was tossed into the raging sea and drowned along with his officers. This is not entirely clear when we look for a direct statement in the text of the Torah. The Song of the Sea in Exodus 15 only makes reference to the king's chariot and cavalry. The account found on the granite *naos* on display in the museum at Ismailia merely states that the pharaoh "was seen no more." *Sepher Ha Yashar* relates that the king actually survived a watery death and finally believed in the God of Israel. This same Midrash goes on to say that the pharaoh was led to Ninevah where he ruled as king.

This description recalls the ninth plague as described found in Chapter 10 of the book of Exodus— a darkness that was palpable in its effect. Verse 22 relates that it lasted three days but does not state that it ended after that period. The great Jewish Bible scholar, the Rambam, teaches that all of the plagues lasted seven days, including the plague of darkness. The first period of darkness fell prior to the death of the first born and lasted six days but the seventh day of total darkness did not occur until Israelites crossed the Sea of Reeds.[1]

Returning to the text of the granite *naos* at Ismailia we learn that the king and his men fight, *"the evil ones at the Place of the Whirlpool."*

The text calls this site ***"Pi-Kharoti,"*** as it relates the frightful fate of the king,

> "There at Pi-Kharoti the Pharaoh is thrown by a whirlwind high into the air and seen no more."

Compare this extraordinary account with the dramatic splitting of the sea found in Exodus 14:9. The Torah teaches that the Children of Israel had made their miraculous passage through *Yam Suf* (Sea of Reeds) while camped at a place called *Pi Ha Khirot*. Notice the similarity of the Egyptian *Pi-Karoti* on the naos and Biblical *Pi-Ha Khirot*.

The monument speaks of a king called **Pharaoh Thoum**. Before he is snatched from their midst, the pharaoh exhorts his men to follow him and promised they would again *find light*. Can this be the Sixth Dynasty king we know as Neferkare the Younger?

We have already learned that pharaohs were known by many names. We must also remember that the vowels found in the translations of the names are little more than educated guesses.

There are two ways to connect Thoum with Neferkare the Younger. The Turin Papyrus lists Neferekare's other name as Nem-**tam**-saf II. This name may have been a shortened form. The latter name does contain the requisite consonants of 't' and 'm' and could be rendered as *'Thoum'*.

We can turn to the works of the Jewish historian Flavius Josephus. He survived the Roman campaigns against Israel and later wrote a history of the Jewish People. It was published around 93 CE. Another of his works was *Against Apion* in which he defends Judaism while taking to task earlier historians, notably the Egyptian Manetho. It is Josephus who preserves some of the words of Manetho that were lost when the Alexandrian Library was destroyed. He does take issue with much of what Manetho says about the Jewish people and rightly so. Manetho's references have a strong anti-Semetic flavor and he freely mixes historical events with fancy to fashion his own case against the Jewish people. However, there is an intriguing name that matches the narrative found on the black granite stone in Ismailia. Manetho writes,

> "There was a king of ours, whose name was **Timaus**. Under him it came to pass, I know not how, that God was averse to us, and there came, after a surprising manner, men of ignoble birth out of the eastern parts, and had boldness

> enough to make an expedition into our country and subdued it by force..."[2]

Josephus quotes Manetho's lengthy rant regarding the invaders. They sound very much like the warring, bloody hordes of Amalek. The people of Amalek are the Bible's first terrorists, attacking the rear guard of the departing Israelites. Manetho labels the invaders as *Hyksos* or Shepherd Kings and states that they held sway over Egypt for five hundred and eleven years. They should not be confused with the Israelites. It must be remembered that no Israelite, not even Joseph, was ever crowned a king of Egypt. Nor did the Israelites take the country by force -- and they certainly did not spend over five hundred years in Egypt. Manetho also reports that *the Hyksos numbered in the thousands when they entered the country by force.*[3] That is a far cry from the mere seventy that comprised the family of Jacob when they arrived to settle in Goshen.

Manetho speaks of his nation falling into decline during the time of a pharaoh called Timaus.[4] This name is very similar to Pharaoh Toum on the black granite *naos*. An additional link to the aforementioned pharaoh Thom can be found in the Torah, in the first chapter of Exodus.

> "Therefore they did set over them taskmasters to afflict them with their burdens. And they built for Pharaoh treasure cities, **Pithom** and Ramases."[5]

The prefix "Pi" can be found attached to other ancient Egyptian cities and roughly translated means "city of" or "dwelling of". The above verse from the book of Exodus could very well be referring to the "**City of Thom**."

Visiting Pithom

On my last trip to Egypt I persuaded our driver to locate the ruins of *Tel al-Muskhuta*. After getting directions we motored from Ismailia a few miles to the west and found a remote dusty village. When we first arrived it appeared that there was little to see. There were a few ancient structures protruding through the arid soil so I powered up my video camera and began to get some footage of the site. Hearing voices from behind me and I turned to see an advancing army of locals. A slender young Arab man sporting a checkered shirt and red baseball cap led the ragged little crowd. "Please!

Archaeologist Nasir Allah standing in front of the ruins at Tel al-Muskhuta (Pithom)

Tel al-Muskhuta, located between the Nile Delta and Lake Timsah, is believed to be Biblical Pithom.

No pictures," he shouted. I reluctantly dropped the camera just as the mob arrived.

The red-capped man was Nasır Allah and claimed to be with the government department of antiquities. He repeated his demand that we not take pictures, but as we began to ask questions about the site he warmed to us. Nasir then led us on an impromptu tour. We followed him back into the center of the village where we saw more ruins uncovered by excavation. Among the walls and ramparts were various piles of pottery and some tools.

"There are no inscriptions yet," Nasir told us, but he pointed to one level of the excavation explaining that he had uncovered evidence of the Persian period and below that remains of a ruin from the 19th Dynasty in the New Kingdom. Nasir went on to say that he was confident they will uncover even older levels of occupation. We also learned from him that there is no funding available for excavation and that he has carried out this work on his own time.

Current excavation at Tel al-Muskhuta (Pithom) has revealed at least two levels of occupation

"This is the way the Egyptian armies would travel…from here back to Memphis," Nasir explained, "this was a garrison to guard the East…in the past it was built by Beni Israel." I was delighted to hear him utter these words. Possibly he is Coptic, which would explain his belief in the Biblical story. For an archaeologist—an Egyptian—to admit this is encouraging to me. When we departed, I turned to request a picture of him because I noticed he stood in front of a ruin. He allowed me a picture and I ask for another. Realizing what I really wanted, Nasir smiled and moved out of the frame, "Please, you may take one picture of the site."

Notes on Chapter Eleven

1 Rabbi Yaakov Culi, *Meam Loez*, Vol. 5, p.20 (Moznaim Publishing 1979)

[2] *Complete Works of Josephus* (Kregel Publications 1981) pp. 610-611

[3] ibid. p.617

[4] this is the Greek form of an Egyptian name...Manetho wrote his History of Egypt in Greek.

[5] Exodus 1:11

CHAPTER TWELVE

Will the Real Mount Sinai Please Stand?

Where is the mountain the Bible alternately calls Sinai and Horeb? It would take another book to completely do justice to this subject and there are already a number of books published that offer a variety of locations for the "Mountain of God". At present, there are about eleven proposed sites for Mount Sinai. Here is a quick survey of the most popular, with my accompanying criteria and my objections.

Jebel Musa

This mountain, elevation 7,497 feet, in the Southern Sinai Peninsula, is best known for St. Catherine's Monastery located at its base. The building was commissioned by Justinian of Constantinople and yielded an early Greek version of the scriptures known as the *Codex Sinaiticus*, found in 1844. *Jebel Musa* is the least likely of all sites because of the ruggedness of the surrounding terrain. It would have been almost impossible for the Israelites to camp among the craggy outcroppings and canyons.[1] It should be remembered that they did indeed encounter hardships along the way but the actual topography of the Sinai range, almost unchanged since the time of the Exodus, would thwart the movement of any large group of travelers.

Jebel Sinn Bishr

A location some 60 miles due east of the present-day Bitter Lakes. Professor Menashe Har-El who began his initial research in 1956 believes this is the most likely location. He decided on *Jebel Sinn Bishr* after climbing ten other mountains in the region. Har-El cites the historical migration of quail near the mountain as one proof. This recalls the incident in Numbers, chapter 11, when Israel complains about the manna, and God sends quail from the sea. Har-El also believes the Arabic name for the site provides another clue because it means "the mountain of the giving of the message".[2] Dr. David Faiman, says that the *Jebel Sinn Bishr* is the Biblical Sinai because it is said to be a three day journey from the Delta region of Egypt. He bases this on Moses' statement to Pharaoh that Israel required a three day trek to worship in the wilderness. However, the real Sinai was certainly more than three days away since a simple reading of Exodus19:1 and Numbers 33:3 reveals that the Twelve Tribes arrived at Mount Sinai *at least 45 days after their initial departure from Egypt.*

Serabit el-Khadem

In antiquity this mountain was situated near the Egyptian copper mines. It could be reached by traveling south and east along the Sinai Peninsula. Among the rocks in this region, Sir Flinders Petrie had discovered pictographs and inscriptions written in what is now termed Proto-Sinaitic.[3] Like the rest of the Sinai, the inhospitable terrain of the area makes it a poor choice for a large mobile encampment. Since there is ample evidence that this was an active mining region and heavily garrisoned by the Egyptians. That might have been reason enough for the Israelites to avoid it.

Jebel al Lawz

Site made popular by Howard Blum's bestselling ***The Gold of the Exodus.*** The book follows the exploits of Larry Williams and Bob Cornuke on their way to *Jebel al Lawz* in Saudi Arabia. Blum's book is a real page-turner but fails badly on Biblical facts. The duo's theory that the Israelites crossed the sea at the Straits of Tiran is based on an imaginary time span. As the two of them got closer to the straits, Cornuke surmised,

> "If the Israelites had gone nineteen days before they came to the Red Sea, then that's more proof the crossing took place a good distance out of Goshen. It supports our theory completely."[4]

Their math is pure speculation and completely ignores what the Jewish sources reveal. *Sefer Ha Yashar* states the Egyptian spies caught up with Israel when they were already camped beside the sea on the **fifth day of the Exodus**.[5] After Pharaoh was given the news he responded by mounting an attack. Israel walks through the divided Reed Sea and the Egyptians are drowned, according to *Seder Ha Olam* on the 21st day of the First month -- seven days into the Exodus.[6]

Remember, the Israelites were instructed to **turn back** toward the Reed Sea so that Pharaoh would believe that they had become lost (see chapter 11 of this book). The path proposed by Williams and Cornuke fails to mention the diversionary tactic of turning back as referenced in Exodus 14:2-3.

Up Against the Wall

Another vital clue ignored by our dangerous duo concerns the *Shur* Wilderness and how it impacted the path taken by Israel as they departed from Egypt. This can get complicated, so pay attention as we establish the general locale of *Shur* and why it is important. Genesis 25:18 reveals that *Shur* was a boundary for the descendants of Ishmael.

> "His descendants lived in the area **from Havilah to Shur, which borders Egypt**, all the way to Assyria. They overran all their brethren."

Initially it might appear that this encompasses modern Saudi Arabia but the final words of the above verse reveal that the Ishmaelites historically have dominated all of the Middle East. It is also important to note that Egypt's western and southern boundaries are unimportant to our thesis because Israel had to leave by heading out either north or east. Egypt's northern boundary has always been the Mediterranean. The Gulf of Suez was another natural barrier. As mentioned earlier, prior to the building of the Suez Canal, the Gulf extended much farther north than it does today.

According to Numbers 33:6-8, Israel entered a region called Etham ***before*** they journeyed to *PiHahiroth* (Freedom Valley). It was at *PiHahiroth* that they would experience the splitting of the sea. After that they would return to Etham. Since this matches the route as described in Exodus 15:22 ("Israel traveled for three days in the Etham Desert and camped in

Marah") we can conclude that Etham and Shur are basically the same region.

> "Moses led the Israelites from the Red Sea and they went out into the Shur Desert. For three days they traveled in the desert without finding water. Finally they came to Marah, but they could not drink the any water there." - Exodus 15:22-23

Here is where *Gold of the Exodus* really runs into a wall. Williams and Cornuke cite the aforementioned Biblical verses. The duo then concludes that the Israelites cross the Straits of Tiran and make their way north in present day Saudi Arabia. But Willliams and Cornuke fail to reference any verse revealing that *Shur* was on the border of Egypt. There are several Biblical passages that lead us to the location of Shur. The book of Genesis details Abraham's decision to move from the plains of Mamre after the utter destruction of Sodom.

> "Abraham migrated from there to the land of the Negev, and he settled between Kadesh and Shur. He would often visit Gerar."- Genesis 20:1

In the chapters that follow, Abraham has dealings with Abimelech, a Philistine king. The patriarch eventually forges a covenant with the king at Beersheva, now in Israel's southern desert, the Negev. Genesis 21:34 states very plainly,

> "Abraham lived there in the land of the Philistines for many days."

Abraham made his home in Philistine-occupied Canaan. It was between Kadesh and Shur.

This is important because the many Biblical references to the Philistines cite their being a coastal people. There is no place in the Bible that we find Philistine influence anywhere near present-day Saudi Arabia.

Compare the two separate accounts of Hagar and Sarah. Hagar was an Egyptian princess who became a handmaiden to Sarah. Hagar gave birth to Ishmael. When Sarah sends them away, the book of Genesis records her fate in two separate passages. Genesis 16:1 relates that it happens while Abraham is living in Canaan.

> "An angel of God encountered her by a spring in the desert, in the oasis, on the road to Shur."
> --Genesis 16:7

Hagar is on the road to Shur. This daughter of Pharaoh has been living in the tent of her master Abraham but she has been sent packing. By any turn of logic she has to be heading back home to Egypt. So she has taken the road to Shur. And why not -- since Shur borders Egypt?

The very same story is related in chapter 21 of Genesis. It begins, in verse 9, telling of Sarah's wish that Hagar and Ishmael be sent away. Reluctantly, Abraham agrees. The mother and child depart.

> "She left and roamed aimlessly in the Beer-sheba desert." – Genesis 21:14

The account continues in the same vein as the 16th chapter of Genesis. Hagar encounters an angel and is told that her son will become a great nation.

I have given a rather lengthy exposition to establish:

- These accounts took place in an area occupied by the Philistines.
- Part of this region is known today as the Negev, specifically near Beersheba.
- The region was between Kadesh and Shur.
- The road to Shur was nearby.
- Shur was a border of Egypt
- The Israelites marched *from the Sea of Reeds into the Desert of Shur.*

By looking at the map and factoring in the above geographical data from the Biblical text we have to conclude that Shur was closer to an area roughly east of the present Suez Canal and not, as Williams and Cornuke would have us believe, somewhere in present day Saudi Arabia.

Even the meaning of the word *Shur* provides another clue as to its location. It is the Hebrew word for "wall." Just after the turn of the century, Egyptologist Heinrich Brugsch-Bey wrote of this wall in his *Egypt Under the Pharaohs.*

"The list of defenses which were intended to protect the country. Still further to the north-east, on the western border of Lake Sirbonis, was another important frontier stronghold, called Anbu, that is,'the wall' or 'rampart'. The Hebrews knew it as *Shur* and the Greeks as *Gherron*. Whoever traveled eastwards out of Egypt was obliged to pass 'the walls' before being allowed to enter the 'way of the Philistines' on his further journey.[7]

He also quotes a tattered papyrus containing the report of a royal scribe who tracks two fugitives from the capitol all the way to Khetam (which is probably the Biblical Etham). The scribe adds that he had missed the two escapees because they had already passed the "ramparts" or "walls" that were near Khetam.[8] These ancient geographic designations seem to offer more evidence that the Desert of Shur was named for a fortified wall that protected Egypt's eastern frontiers, near the Way of the Philistines. It also convinces me that the Israelite camp did not take the route suggested by Williams and Cornuke.

But the author, Howard Blum, also gets low marks for poor research. He writes Israel took "three arduous months"[9] to reach Sinai. This reveals a misunderstanding of the Biblical text. Exodus 19:1 states that Israel and their camp arrived ***on the first day*** of the Third month. Rabbi Nathan Bushwich in his *Understanding the Jewish Calendar* states that a month is simply defined as the time between the appearance of one new moon to the next...an average of 29 ½ days.[10] And since the Hebrews departed from Egypt on the 15th day of the

First month and arrived at Sinai on the 1st day of the Third month **only 45 days had elapsed.**

It is vital to remember that it was only five days later that the Torah (the Ten Commandments or Ten Utterances) was given to Moses. This was the 50th day. It has been celebrated for thousands of years as the Jewish feast *Shavuoth,* literally "weeks" and coincides with one of three annual harvest festivals that Israel is commanded to keep.

> "Shavuot commemorates the awesome event experienced by the Children of Israel **seven weeks after their exodus** from Egypt."[11]

You Can't Get There From Here

All of the aforementioned sites do not meet a simple acid test found in the text of the Torah. You will recall that as the Hebrews, along with the mixed multitude, departed from Egypt they were instructed not to take the most accessible route—although it was nearer.

Ultimately, the Promised Land would be Israel's final destination, but their **first stop** was always Mount Sinai where they would receive the Torah. Many of the commandments given in the Torah are conditional on their being in the Land of Israel and are preceded with the phrase, "When you enter the land."[12] So, there was a genuine prerequisite for Revelation at Sinai. The Twelve Tribes and mixed multitude were to receive instruction before their arrival at the borders of Israel. Their Bill of Rights, Constitution and Deed were all wrapped up in the Torah. The above verse makes it clear that the more direct path was along the ancient Philistine Highway, running along the Mediterranean coast. None of the aforementioned sites are reached by taking that route.

An Italian archaeologist, Professor Immanuel Anati, offers another possible location for Mount Sinai in Israel's Negev desert, just four miles from the Egyptian border. The site is called *Har Karkom*. After crossing the Sea of Reeds, the Israelites generally traveled in an easterly direction, arriving at *Har Karkom* (Mt. Saffron). If Israel took such a route they would naturally be approaching the site from the west. It is interesting to note that the mountain can only be reached by traversing a large valley to the west of Karkom.

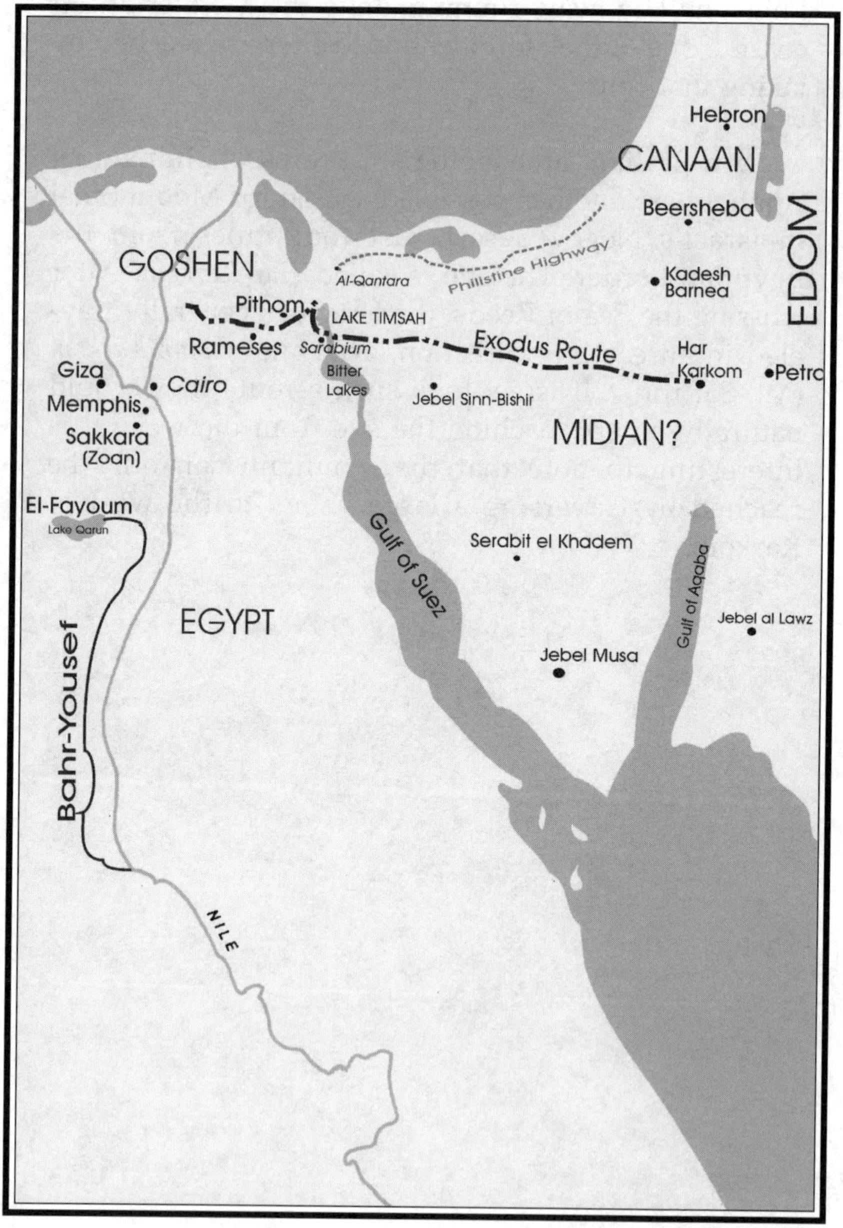
Hebron
CANAAN
Beersheba
EDOM
GOSHEN
Al-Qantara
Philistine Highway
Kadesh Barnea
Pithom
LAKE TIMSAH
Rameses
Sarabium
Exodus Route
Har Karkom
Petra
Giza
Cairo
Bitter Lakes
Jebel Sinn-Bishir
Memphis
Sakkara (Zoan)
MIDIAN?
El-Fayoum
Lake Qarun
Gulf of Suez
Serabit el Khadem
Gulf of Aqaba
Jebel al Lawz
EGYPT
Jebel Musa
Bahr-Yousef
NILE

Notes on Chapter Twelve

[1] A figure of millions of departing slaves is easily determined when you extrapolate the number of 600,000 fighting men, as cited in the Torah, accompanied by their wives, children and grandparents.

[2] Sue Fishkoff, *Looking for Mt. Sinai*, (Jerusalem Post International Edition, October 19, 1996)p.20

[3] Ian Wilson, *The Bible is History* (Weidenfeld & Nicolson, London 1999) p.58-60

[4] Blum, *The Gold of Exodus* (Pocketbooks, New York, 1998) pp.23-214

[5] Book of Jasher (Artisan Press, Muskogee, Oklahoma) p.229

[6] Rabbi Shlomo Rotenburg, *Am Olam* (Feldheim Books, Spring Valley, NY, 1988) p.49

[7] Brugsch-Bey, *Egypt Under the Pharaohs* (Bracken Books, London, 1902) p.97

[8] ibid, p. 320

[9] Blum, *The Gold of Exodus* (Pocket Books, NY, 1998) p.304

[10] Bushwick, *Understanding the Jewish Calendar* (Moznaim Publishers, New York, 1989) p.5

[11] Rabbi Hayim Halevy Donin, *To Be a Jew* (Basic Books, New York, 1972) p.239

[12] For just a few examples see Ex 12:25, Ex.32:13, Ex.14:34, Lev.19:23, Num.15:2, Num.34:1

CHAPTER THIRTEEN
The Mountain of God

Har Karkom (Mount Saffron), in Israel's Negev Desert, is some thirty miles from the Egyptian border. The site is thick with evidence of cultural occupation dating back thousands of years.

Professor Anati was the first to seriously consider *Har Karkom* in the 1950's and has since conducted extensive research in the region which is roughly sixty miles from the nearest human habitation. In 1986, after several international expeditions, Anati published his findings in ***The Mountain of God***. Prior to the book's release, writing in *Bible Archaeology Review,* Professor

Anati tells why he found the site so intriguing, as well as the typical response from other academics.

> "One of the greatest living Bible scholars twitted me for exaggerating the significance of *Har Karkom*. The whole Sinai Peninsula and the Negev were probably full of holy mountains, he told me, so we should not be bothered trying to identify *Har Karkom* in the Bible. To this I reacted very strongly; there was something wrong in this approach. I knew Sinai and the Negev very well. I had worked there for 30 years. I had never seen another mountain with such a tremendous amount of evidence of worship and of tribal gatherings as *Har Karkom*. It was hard for me to believe that such a site would not be mentioned in the Bible."[1]

Karkom is interesting for the number of ancient rock carvings executed by large groups who obviously had some time on their hands. Some of the rock art even depicts the stones engraved with the Ten Commandments. It is also rich in cultural evidence such as stone monuments and what appear to be altars surrounding the mountain.

> "This mountain and its surroundings have revealed to date over 400 archaeological sites, although it is situated in the middle of a wasteland that has otherwise provided us with very few archaeological remains during our quite thorough survey of the surrounding area."[2]

Anati remarks on the amazing quantity of these surrounding sites that mark the mountain as a setting frequented by pilgrims, even from antiquity. Many of the pieces of rock art depict people in worship. The many ruins and evidence of settlements at *Karkom* are notable for matching the descriptions found in the Torah for certain landmarks. For instance, Anati discovered twelve pillars erected near the mountain.

> "This group of 12 pillars and the platform nearby vaguely reminded me of a passage in the Bible. I went on to our camp and took out a Bible and found the passage: 'And Moses...rose up early in the morning, and builded an altar under the hill, and 12 pillars, according to the 12 tribes of Israel' (Exodus 24:4)"[3]

At the top of *Karkom*, Anati discovered a small cave. He points out that the desert region is full of such caves -- but they are a rarity on the mountaintops of the region. This small cave vividly recalls Exodus 33:22 where Moses is granted a request to view the glory of God and is placed within the cleft of a rock for his protection. In addition to the evidence of numerous dwellings all over the site, there is also an abundant supply of water. Anati even found a well and what appeared to be small man-made channels that connect water holes at the foot of *Karkom*.

Though Professor Anati is convinced that *Har Karkom* meets much of the criteria for being the Biblical Mount Sinai, I have a real problem with his dating methodology. He says that archaeological evidence proves that Karkom was uninhabited during the popularly accepted dating of the Exodus. Anati theorizes that the cultural remains found in the region can be dated to as far back as 80,000 BC! I am confounded when competent, intelligent researchers attach these kind of dates to archaeological sites that are exposed to the ravages of the elements as they are at *Karkom*.

Notes on Chapter Thirteen

[1] Anati, *Has Mt. Sinai Been Found?* (BAR, July/August 1985) p.54

[2] ibid, p. 47

[3] ibid, p. 54

CHAPTER FOURTEEN

Dating the Exodus

"Judaism is a religion of time, aiming at the sanctification of time...Judaism teaches us to be attached to the holiness in time, to be attached to sacred events..." - Abraham Joshua Heschel

Hopefully, we have demonstrated a logical connection between the Biblical Exodus story and the end of the Old Kingdom period in Egypt. Now, we should be able to pinpoint this pivotal event in time. But whose chronology should we consult? The timetables of other cultures of the Near East and even our own calendars have all been subjected to constant revision. However, the Jewish historical chronology, known as *Seder Ha Olam,* differs from secular timetables in one important respect. It has *never* changed. Commemorating events and keeping time permeates the worship of Judaism beginning with marking the Sabbath as the seventh day. The above quoted religious philosopher, Heschel, eloquently expresses this idea as he relates how holiness was attached, at the very beginning, to time.

"Now what was the first holy object in the history of the world? Was it a mountain? Was it an altar? It is, indeed, a unique occasion at which the distinguished word *kadosh* (holy) is used for the first time: in the Book of Genesis at the end of the story of creation. How extremely significant is the fact that it is applied to time: 'And God

> blessed the seventh day and made it holy' [Gen.2:3]. There is no reference in the record of creation to any object in space that would be endowed with the quality of holiness."[1]

God reinforces this concept by commanding Israel to remember the seventh day *to keep it holy*.

The Jewish year revolves around holy festivals such as Sukkoth, Rosh Ha Shanah, Yom Kippur and, of course, Passover. It is incumbent on God's people to track time. Their very survival depends on it. So it is not surprising that the Jewish people have kept a meticulous record of their very origins. They can trace milestones in their history to the month and day. The events as cataloged in *Seder Ha Olam* reckon the flow of years from the first man, Adam. For example, the year 1948 would be 5708 or five thousand seven hundred eight years from Adam. The Exodus? The date of the first Passover, marking the freedom from slavery of the Israelite people is still memorialized as the 15th day of first month (now called Nissan) in the year 2448. This and other pivotal dates can be found in *Seder Ha Olam*.

My reference for the *Seder Ha Olam* comes from the impressive work of Eliezer Shulman who published an English language version, in the form of charts and tables, as *The Sequence of Events in the Old Testament.* Shulman carried out this remarkable work while exiled in Siberia. With much time on his hands, he studied his copy of *Seder Ha Olam,* the *Tanakh,* and other Jewish sources to compute the many dates and genealogies as recorded in the Bible. Comparing these figures to those in *Seder Ha Olam* revealed a seamless

Timetable of History
(based on *Seder Ha Olam*)

Event	Jewish Chronology	Gregorian Date
Death of Adam	930	2830 BCE
Birth of Noah	1056	2704 BCE
Birth of Shem	1558	2204 BCE
The Flood	1656	2104 BCE
Birth of Abraham	1948	1812 BCE
Peleg dies, Earth divided, Tower falls	1996	1764 BCE
Death of Noah	2006	1754 BCE
Birth of Isaac	2048	1712 BCE
Death of Abraham's father, Terah	2083	1683 BCE
The Binding of Isaac, death of Sarah	2085	1675 BCE
Birth of Jacob & Esau	2108	1652 BCE

Event	Jewish Chronology	Gregorian Date
Abraham dies, Esau kills Nimrod, sells the birthright to Jacob	2123	1637 BCE
Shem, son of Noah dies	2158	1602 BCE
Jacob marries Leah	2192	1568 BCE
Birth of Levi	2195	1564 BCE
Birth of Joseph	2199	1561 BCE
Joseph becomes Vizier of Egypt	2229	1531 BCE
Jacob and his family settle in Goshen	2238	1522 BCE
Jacob dies in Egypt	2255	1505 BCE
Joseph dies in Egypt	2309	1451 BCE
Levi dies and the Hebrews are enslaved	2332	1428 BCE
Moses is born	2368	1392 BCE
Exodus	2448	1312 BCE

corridor in time through the ages to the present.

Consulting this timetable gives us some remarkable insights to the events recorded in the Torah. For instance, we learn the flood of Noah had taken place 1656 years from Adam. Three hundred forty years later, in 1996, the continents shifted apart, an event that also caused the fall of the Tower of Babel.[2]

> "Eber had two sons. The name of the first was Peleg, because the world became divided in his days - Genesis 10:25

Abraham was only forty-eight years of age at the time and was witness to the massive tectonic activity that split the continents

The chronology spans the years from creation right through the Diaspora. I have only listed a few of the dates from the death of Adam up until the Exodus. A complete listing from *Seder Ha Olam* is outside the scope of this book, but I wanted to mark some of the milestones from this amazing timetable. I have also listed the years as they occur on our present calendar. Take the time to compare some of the dates and discover for yourself some very intriguing revelations. You will note that Jacob and Esau were only fifteen years old at the time that Esau sold his birthright for a mess of pottage.

Another important lesson drawn from this chronology is the actual number of years of exile promised to Abraham's descendants. This is critical to any study of the Exodus. Scholars often stumble over this vital point. At one place, the Biblical text seems to relate that from the time that Jacob and his family arrived in Egypt until the day that Moses brought the Israelites out of bondage was four hundred years. At yet another point in the Book of Exodus, it seems to state clearly that Israel spent four hundred thirty years. The Oral Tradition teaches that the Egyptian exile only lasted two hundred ten years. At first glance it would seem that we have three contradictory times spans. However, as you will see, all three are correct.

At the beginning of chapter fifteen of Genesis, as Abram sacrifices three kosher animals, God makes a promise to the patriarch.[3] Note also that the patriarch is still called Abram and he has not yet fathered Isaac.

> "God said to Abram, 'Know for sure that your descendants will be foreigners in a land that is not theirs for four hundred years. They will be enslaved and oppressed. But I will finally bring judgment against the nation who enslaves them, and they will then leave with great wealth.'" – Genesis 15:13

The language of God's promise to Abraham can be divided into three time periods and three levels of exile.

- Abraham's seed would be a *ger* (a foreigner) in a land not theirs.

- They would be *abad* (a worker)

- They would be *anah* (oppressed, humbled) and depart with wealth.

If we look at the lives of Abraham's son and grandson, Isaac and Jacob we can see that the words of Genesis 15:13 were fulfilled. Isaac was always a foreigner, leading an almost nomadic life. Isaac was sixty when Jacob was born.[4]

In the case of Jacob, his years working under his shifty uncle Laban could definitely be characterized as humbling servitude. And when Jacob departed, in haste, he had become a man of substance. Jacob's experiences would be the template for the events in the lives of his descendants. Jacob also relocated several times and eventually settled in Egypt when his son Joseph became viceroy. Jacob was one hundred thirty when he arrived in Egypt.[5]

God told Abraham that his offspring would be a stranger, so the counting of the 400 years *begins with the birth of his son, Isaac:.*

From Isaac's birth	
until the birth of Jacob	60 years
From Jacob's birth	
until his arrival in Egypt:	+130 years
	190 years

210 years of exile remain for the descendants of Abraham. We can determine the 400 year exile by taking the above figures and adding them:

Number of years from the birth of Isaac unti Jacob enters Egypt	190 years
Actual length of exile	+210 years
	400 years

Seder Ha Olam gives us an exact chronology based on the years as recorded in the exile.

Exile begins when Jacob and his entire household migrate to Egypt	2238
Exodus from Egypt occurs with the departure of Israel from Egypt	- 2448
Subtract the difference from these dates and you get:	210

Is there a contradiction between the four hundred years mentioned in Genesis 15:13 and the four hundred thirty year span in the following verse?

> "The lifestyle that the Israelites endured in Egypt had thus lasted 430 years. At the end of 430 years, all of God's armies left Egypt in broad daylight." – Exodus 12:40

There is no discrepancy according to Seder Ha Olam. It reveals that the added thirty years is reckoned by counting from the time that *the promise was given to Abraham...a promise made thirty years before the birth of Isaac.* Rabbi Aryeh Kaplan's use of the word "lifestyle" is a more accurate rendering of the text. If I may be allowed to further clarify the text, it could be understood in the following manner:

> "Israel endured a life of exile while in Egypt. That kind of existence had begun 430 years earlier when Abraham began his life in exile."

Notes on Chapter Fourteen

[1] Heschel, *The Sabbath* (Farrar Straus & Young, NY, 1951) p. 6

[2] Shulman, *Sequence of Events in the Old Testament* (Ministry of Defense Publishing, Israel 1987) p.21

[3] These same animals would later be used in the Temple offerings.

[4] Genesis 25:26

[5] Genesis 47:9

CONCLUSION

CHAPTER FIFTEEN
Remembering Joseph

The story of the Exodus really began with Joseph. Had this son of Jacob not been sold into slavery and eventually come to rule Egypt there could not have been an Exodus. The last chapter of the book of Genesis relates how God used Joseph to not only save his own people but the entire nation of Egypt from starvation.

The wisdom granted Joseph allowed him to enrich the throne and to build Egypt into a world empire. We are told in the Torah that he was called *Zafanth PaAnnekh,* a title that meant he was a revealer of secrets. These secrets were not only the hidden things of the cosmos they were what we call technology. Surely his achievements must have found their way into the annals of Egypt. If we have shown that the Exodus occurred at the end of the Sixth Dynasty, we should be able to find evidence of Joseph in one of the previous dynasties.

In the Third Dynasty, during the reign of the Pharaoh known as *Djoser,* we find a noble figure that exhibits amazing talents. He was called *Imhotep.* He was a competent administrator for the crown but he apparently excelled in architecture and medicine.

The wise Imhotep is believed to have designed the famous Step Pyramid of Djoser at Sakkara

Imhotep is best known today as the designer of the famous Step Pyramid at Saqqara. Could this be Joseph?

Two additional facts make *Imhotep* a strong contender for the Biblical Joseph. Remember how Joseph saved Egypt from a famine that would last for seven years? Inscribed on a rock near the first cataract of the Nile, at Sehel, is the account from the time of King *Djoser*. The inscription relates that pharaoh was deeply distressed because of a seven-year famine. He sought the counsel of the wise *Imhotep*.

A Chamber found at Saqqara, close to the famous Step Pyramid may belong to *Imhotep*.. The tomb is interesting because it was never completed. If Joseph was, indeed, the legendary designer of the pyramid it might account for the unfinished state of the monument. We know from the Bible that Joseph was only interred on a temporary basis. Genesis 50:25 relates his deathbed wish that his remains be carried out of Egypt when God remembered His promise to the Children of Israel to free them from exile and lead them into their own land. At Bet Khallaf in Upper Egypt, *Djoser* appears alongside another individual called *Zanakht*. No pyramid has ever been found for *Zanakht* and it has been suggested that the Step Pyramid may have been originally intended for him.[1] Could *Zanakht* be a linguistic corruption of Joseph's title, *Zafanth PaAnnekh,* as found in Genesis 41:45?

Joseph and *Imhotep* also share another remarkable similarity...they both lived to the ripe old age of 110. There was a proverb passed down through the centuries among the Egyptians. It was said that to achieve perfect wisdom one should live to the age of 110.

According to Arab historians, when Joseph was 100, he was asked by younger, envious court officials to prove his worth by converting a stretch of arid desert into fertile ground. He amazed Pharaoh and his rivals by engineering a feeder canal from the Nile to create a

Bahr-Yousef, the "Sea of Joseph" still irrigates a region west of the Nile called the El-Fayoum.

Lake Qarun, fed by Bahr-Yousef is part of an ancient man-made oasis called the El-Fayoum.

body of water that would provide irrigation for the parched desert.

Today, southwest of modern Cairo is *Birqet Qarun*, a large, freshwater lake in a natural basin. This region, called the *El Fayoum*, is actually a man-made oasis. An ancient canal that has existed since the days of the Pharaohs feeds the lake. Since antiquity that waterway has been called *Bahr Yousef:* the Sea of Joseph.

There is another possibility for our Joseph.

The Inscription of Weni

In 1860, digging in the dusty vaults of Abydos, Auguste Mariette found a stone slab inscribed with the events in the life of a nobleman called *Weni*. He came from humble birth and was raised to one of the most exalted positions in all of Egypt as Viceroy to at least three Pharaohs. He was so trusted by the king that he was enlisted to hear cases involving secret matters in the King's harem. The king's trust in this matter recalls Joseph's own experience with his master's wife. He would not succumb her charms, even though it meant the dungeon for him.

Among the other accomplishments of *Weni* was the engineering of a series of canals fed by the Nile. He also waged war with the so-called Sand Dwellers. These exploits are remarkably similar to those of Joseph as told in *Sefer Ha Yashar*. It recounts Joseph's military campaign for pharaoh in the Land of Havilah and his victories there against the people of Tarshish.

According to the Inscription of *Weni*, he lived during the reigns of Teti, Pepi I and Merenre. Some Egyptologist are troubled that *Weni* would have been well over 60 years of age by the time he entered the service of Merenre. But, *Sefer Ha Yashar* relates that Joseph was 71 years of age when a pharaoh, called Magron, took the throne.

The inscription of Weni. He was Vizier or Prime Minister to at least three pharaohs during the Old Kingdom era.

Which of these legendary figures is Joseph? Is it *Imhotep* or is it *Weni*?

I propose that they are one and the same.

We noted earlier that the Old Kingdom had been a period of remarkable stability. With such a strong government positioned in Memphis for the Third, Fourth and Sixth Dynasty it makes no sense to move the seat of power hundreds of miles south to Elephantine during the Fifth Dynasty and then back to Memphis. The pharaohs of the Third and Fourth Dynasties could have ruled from Memphis while the kings listed in the Fifth Dynasty from Elephantine were actually their contemporaries serving as co-regents.

By aligning the Fourth and Fifth Dynasties we also shorten the span of time between the Third Dynasty ruler *Djoser* and Sixth Dynasty king Merenre, thus allowing our Joseph/*Imhotep*/*Weni* to serve all of them.

There is room for such an alignment. Remember, the catalog of Kings are drawn from sources such as the List at Abydos, The Turin Papyrus, the Tablets at Sakkara, the Palermo Stone and Manetho? Egyptologist Barbara Mertz points out,

> "In some cases we cannot see any evidence that a particular royal line ended where Manetho says it did."[2]

This list is probably inflated due to the possibility that some names are those of princes and other nobles. The chart on the following page is taken from the *Cambridge Ancient History* (1971) and is not immune to conjecture, opinion, agendas and other forms of scholarly meddling.

Joseph would serve as viceroy for 80 years. That length of time would have allowed Joseph to be in

King	Length of Reign
3rd Dynasty	
Nebka	19
Djoser	19
Teti	6
Tuni	24
4th Dynasty	
Sneferu	24
Cheops	23
Redjedef	8
Chephren	25(?)
Baufre (Years of his reign are missing from lists)	(?)
Mycerinus (This span is in doubt)	28
Sepsekaf	4
Dedefptah (name is missing from some lists)	2
5th Dynasty (Ruling from Elephantine)	
Userkaf	7
Sahure	14
Neferirkare	10
Shepseskare	7
Neferefe	7 (?)
Nyuserre	31
Menkauhor	8
Djedkare	39
Unas	30
6th Dynasty	
Teti(aka Othoes)	12
Userkare	1 (/)
Phiops I (aka Pepi 1, some say he was the older brother of Pepi II)	49
Merenre (aka Nemtimsaf I)	14
Phiops II (aka Pepi II, Neferkare, Merire)	94
Merenre II (aka Nemtimsaf II, Neferkare the Younger)	1
Netjerykare	(?)
Nitocris (aka Menkara, Netiqerti)	12 (?)

the service of a king from Elephantine called *Unas*. In Saqqara, near the pyramid of *Unas* there is a causeway featuring various scenes carved in low relief. The most curious of these is block of limestone with a relief featuring starving foreigners. Since the relief is not carved in hieroglyphs, the pictorial is meant to commemorate some important event that sounds very much like the seven years of famine as described in Genesis.

> "Unfortunately this unique scene is incomplete and it is difficult to imagine it context; even the nationality of the figures cannot be identified with a certainty. Since, however, tomb reliefs depicted only incidents or events which the dead owner wished to perpetuate, it must be supposed that the starving people were not Egyptians and that the missing portion contains scenes of provisions being sent to them by *Unas*."[3]

In the tomb of *Unas* there is a startling inscription on the east wall of the antechamber of his burial place. Typically, the virtues of the dead pharaoh are inscribed along with words of praise for him as he carries out various tasks alongside Re, Atum and the other gods of Egypt. The most curious line on this east wall reads as follows,

> "*Unas* will judge with Him-whose-name-is-hidden on the day of the slaying of the eldest"[4]

Is it possible that the aging vizier Joseph, during one of his audiences with this pharaoh, told the king that the Egyptians would one day forget what Joseph had done—how he saved the nation from starvation? In the final chapter of the book of Genesis, Joseph's deathbed promise to ensure that the departing Children of Israel would transport his remains demonstrates that he was fully assured that the Exodus would occur. He could have revealed all of this to *Unas*, telling him that judgment would come on Egypt's first-born as a result of the nation's crimes against Joseph's people. The death of the first-born, the eldest, would come at the hands of a God whose name would never be uttered in the presence of pharaoh. To Pharaoh, a worshipper in many gods, the God of Joseph would most certainly be "Him-whose-name-is-hidden."

It was this deathbed oath that would provide Moses with one of the proofs that he was indeed the deliverer sent by God to bring Israel out of bondage. Joseph's final words are very appropriate for a man known as a "revealer of secrets". He provided his surviving brothers with a coded phrase that they were to pass down to the tribal leaders. They were to look for the coming of one who knew the secret phrase because it would mark him as their deliverer.

> "Joseph then bound the Israelites by an oath: When God grants you special providence you must bring my remains out of this place. " – Genesis 50:25

The text employs the phrase *pakod yifkod* and it is the first time these words appear in the Bible. As with all of the Torah there are several permutations found in the meaning of the words. *Pakod yifkod* can imply paying a debt or in another context, to keep an appointment. We could expand the meaning of the above scripture to express that God would keep his word, at the appointed time, at the end of the 400 years from Isaac. There was a tradition among the Israelite leadership that the true redeemer would know a variation of this phrase as *pakod pakad-ti.* At the Burning Bush, the Creator instructed Moses in this secret code.

> "Go, gather the elders of Israel, and say to them, 'YHVH, The God of your fathers, appeared to me—the God of Abraham, Isaac and Jacob. He said, ' I have granted you special providence [*pakod pakad-ti*] regarding what is happening to you in Egypt.'" - Exodus 3:16

We have reached a place in present day history in which the Jews are facing an appointment. But how can they can they keep that appointment if they do not call it to mind. They must see the Exodus experience as a genuine turning point in time that culminated in the giving of the Torah.

Ultimately, it is this occurrence at Sinai as witnessed by literally millions of Jews that sets them apart as a nation ordained by God. They are to be priesthood and it is their holy task to minister to the needs of the entire planet. May God grant it speedily in our time.

Notes on Chapter Fifteen

[1] Sir Alan Gardiner, *Egypt of the Pharaohs* (Oxford University Press, London) p.74

2 Barbara Mertz, *Temples, Tombs and Hieroglyphs* (Peter Bedrick Books, New York, 1990)p.40

[3] Eugene Strouhal, *Life of the Ancient Egyptians*, (University of Oklahoma Press, Norman)p.187

[4] Miriam Lichtheim, *Ancient Egyptian Literature, Vol. 1: TheOld Kingdom and Middle Kingdom* (University of California Press, Berkeley 1975)p.36-37

THE REST OF THE STORY

APPENDIX A:
Truth Shall Spring From the Earth

A quick glance at any map of the ancient Near East will instantly reveal that Israel was at the crossroads of the two major ancient trade routes. This put the Hebrews in the crosshairs of the known world's political power struggles. Whenever Israel failed to heed God's warnings, through his prophets, the nation's fate would seesaw with the ebb and flow of world empires of Assyria, Babylon, Persia, Rome and, of course, Egypt. The fact that the Bible specifically names these empires and their leaders adds weight to our case for historical veracity. Israel's experience with the warring Assyrians is a good example. The Biblical text is rich with references to the likes of Tiglath-Pileser, Shalmanezer, Sargon, Sennacherib and Esarhaddon. They are all Assyrian tyrants whose campaigns are well known to the casual student of history. One can just as easily call up the many ancient Assyrian texts that confirm the Biblical record. The focus of this is on Egypt. Here is one such reference from the annals of of Tiglath-Pileser,

> "The land of Bit-Humria...all of its people together with their goods I carried off to Assyria. Pakaha, their king I deposed and I placed Ausi over them as king."[1]

The reference to the land of Bit-Humria is actually *the land of the House of Omri* while Pakaha and Ausi are Pekah and Hoshea found in 2nd Kings 15:29.

"In the days of Pekah king of Israel came Tiglathpileser king of Assyria, and took Ijon, and Abelbethmaachah, and Janoah, and Kedesh, and Hazor, and Gilead, and Galilee, all the land of Naphtali, and carried them captive to Assyria. And Hoshea the son of Elah made a conspiracy against Pekah the son of Remaliah, and smote him, and slew him, and reigned in his stead, in the twentieth year of Jotham the son of Uzziah."[2]

The land of Israel encompasses a small patch of the Middle East, but its history is vast. Within the borders of this tiny country (about the size of Delaware) one can find well over twenty-five archaeological sites under excavation during the dig season. Once a year a catalogue of these digs is listed in *Biblical Archaeology Review*.[3] A casual glance will quickly disclose that most of these digs are uncovering physical evidence of people that inhabit the ancient world of the Bible.

Excavations at El Ahwat and Ashkelon reveal proof of Canaanite occupation. Hazor, torched by the armies of Joshua, continues to yield intriguing finds.[4] In 1996, Archaeologist Amnon Ben Tor stood above an ancient floor burnt black and told David Briggs of the Associated Press,

"Hazor was destroyed by fire. Nobody can prove to me that the story in Joshua is entirely fiction."[5]

Excavations in Jerusalem, Qumran, Tiberius, Meggido, Tel Dan, Tamar, and many other locations are a rich source of finds that offer exciting proof of the Bible's authenticity as an historical document. The 1986 discovery of a Biblical text dating to around 600 BCE supports the view that it is a genuine record and not concocted centuries after the events recorded in its pages.[6] Is there physical evidence that supports the text of the Bible? Here are just a few of startling examples of key figures and events that are mentioned in the Bible, now documented through archaeological finds:

Deir Allah

In Chapter 22 of Numbers, as the Israelites journey to the Promised Land they travel through Moab, which is present day Jordan. When confronted with the sight of millions of Israelites moving across the land, the Moabite king Balak hires a great sorcerer to curse Israel. He employs Balaam, the son of Beor to curse the people of Israel. In a night vision, God warns Balaam against cursing His people.[7]

In the biblical account, this prophet is hired apparently due to his great reputation. In fact he travels all the way from his home in Pethor, somewhere in Mesopotamia. Though he is hired to curse the Twelve Tribes, Balaam can only bless the nation of Israel.

Discovered in 1967 at Deir Allah, just north of the Jabbok River in present day Jordan, is an ancient sanctuary and within its walls were found an intriguing inscription preserved in brittle lime plaster. The fading words warn of calamity and the wrath of the gods. The most intriguing aspect of the text is the source of these warnings.

While digging for Professor H. J. Franken, an Arab foreman found the pale ink inscription on the nearly disintegrated plaster. This detail in itself was significant. Writing on a wash of lime-plaster is described in the book of Deuteronomy, Chapter 27. When the Israelites cross over the Jordan into the Promised Land, they are commanded to write the words of the Torah on stones. They are instructed to inscribe the words of the Law on stones and further instructed to plaster them with plaster.[8]

The inscription found at Deir Alla most resembles Aramaic and contains a prophetic warning ending with a prediction of "destruction and ruins." However, the most intriguing aspect of these words of doom is their source. According to the ancient text, found on the wall at Deir Allah, the words are those of Balaam son of Beor.[9]

Jericho

The book of Joshua describes the first military campaign in the land of Canaan after Israel's forty years in the wilderness. It was against the city of Jericho. Joshua 6:1-24 relates how the *Kohanim,* the Priests, carrying the Ark of the Covenant, march around the city for six days. On the seventh day the *shofar* (ram's horn) was blown, all the people shouted and the walls of Jericho fell. Joshua destroyed the city by fire and put every one of its inhabitants to the sword, except for the household of Rahab the harlot.

Tel-Jericho was first excavated in 1868 by Charles Warren and then again in 1930 by John Garstang. Because of the extensive signs of what he called "conflagration and destruction", Garstang was convinced the masses of cracked building stones and charred timbers all pointed to one thing: this was Jericho of the Bible and it had fallen in the manner described in the book of Joshua.[10] In the 1950's, Kathleen Kenyon conducted further research. She felt the pottery found in the ruins did not support the generally accepted date of the Israelite conquest.

Recently, author Bryant Wood reexamined the data from these excavations and concluded that the city's fall was remarkably similar to the Biblical account.[11] Wood found that three walls protected ancient Jericho. The first barrier was a revetment wall about fifteen feet high. Behind that was a sloping rampart that had been plastered smooth making it difficult for attackers to scale, and finally there was the city's upper wall, which served as the third fortification.

One of the first digs at Jericho led by Sellin and Watzinger had found the remains of mud houses behind the first barrier, the revetment wall. These houses were poorly constructed and located away from city's main walls. Wood believes that because they managed to survive the fall of Jericho and appeared to be on the "wrong side of town" that the site could very well be the neighborhood of Rahab the harlot whose home was spared.[12]

The Amarna Letters

An Egyptian peasant woman found the Amarna Tablets in 1887. She was digging near her village of el-Amarna and stumbled onto a cache of nearly 400 clay tablets that formed a library of correspondence to Pharaoh Amenophis III and his son, Akhenaten. Some of the letters are complaints from a warlord in Hebron called Shurwadata. Since he was under the protection of the Egyptian crown, he was seeking relief from a warring tribe he called the *Habiru*.

An ancient collection of letters sent to Pharaoh Akhenaten and his father, Amenophis III, comprise the famous Amarna texts. The clay tablets mention a people called Habiru and a city in Canaan called Urusalim.

In *Pharaohs & Kings,* author David Rohl makes a very convincing case that several of the letters to the Pharaoh are from none other than King Saul. Amarna Tablet number 366 even contains what is very likely a report of the death of Saul as written by the Philistine leader at Gath.[13]

Linguistically *Habiru* is very similar in sound and meaning to the word *Hebrew*. Both words are variously translated to denote a sojourner or wanderer. The word is probably related to the Akkadian *habaru*, which means, "to migrate."[14] The word can be traced to *Eber*, ancestor of the Twelve Tribes and means to "cross over". It is quite possible that our English word "over" comes from this ancient root.

The Amarna tablets are written in Akkadian cuneiform. It was a popular form of communication in the time of Akhenaten in much the same way that English is employed all over the world in much diplomatic correspondence today. In addition, the texts provide a sampling of Biblical place names with references to Meggido, Gaza, Ashkelon, Ashdod, Aiyilon, and Hazor. Of particular interest is a city called *Urusalem*, which is mentioned on six of the tablets. In the Hebrew tongue, Jerusalem would be *Yirushalam*.

Shiloh

The impact of the giving of the Torah cannot be diminished. Of equal importance was the building of the *Mishkhan*,[15] or Tabernacle that housed the Ark of the Covenant. Its design incorporated an abundance of mystical teachings. The Tabernacle is also an abstract representation of the perfected person. The symbolism is simple yet profound. Since the tabernacle is a portable instrument of worship, so is man. Indeed, the Tabernacle would move with the nation of Israel through its desert experience for forty years. After the Twelve Tribes crossed the Jordan, the Tabernacle rested at Gilgal, east of Jericho, for fourteen years as Israel conquered Canaan and settled the land. Afterwards it was moved to the center of a hilly region to a site called Shiloh. The Tabernacle would stand at that site for three hundred forty-nine years.

Shiloh was rediscovered in the 1830's by American explorer and Bible scholar Edward Robison and first excavated by a team from Denmark some years later. Israel Finkelstein, an Israeli archaeologist, has carried out the most extensive research beginning in the 1980's. Today, the nearby modern community of Shiloh continues to develop the site as a tourist attraction.

The Tel Dan Fragment

For years scholars dismissed the existence of the heroic King David. A triangular piece of basalt uncovered in 1993, in northern Israel dealt a blow to the minimalist chant that David was the stuff of myth. The fragment was first spotted by Gila Cook, a surveyor working with Professor Avraham Biran at the dig site in northern Israel.[16] This discovery is not only pivotal to the issue of the Bible's authenticity, but underscores the reality of its people and places in a time when even some secular Israeli historians are questioning their nation's ancient roots.

Written in archaic Hebrew, the stone verifies the personage of *David Ha Melech* and his dynasty known as the House David with the words, *Beit David.* The inscription has been dated to around the 9th Century BCE and commemorates a victory by a neighboring ruler over Israel.[17] Seymour Gitin at the Albright Institute of Archaeological Research in Jerusalem called the Tel Dan Fragment, *"one of the greatest finds of the 20th Century."*[18] The words found on the Tel Dan fragment form the first direct piece of evidence verifying a figure esteemed among all Bible readars, Christians and Jews alike. Even more important, there is apparently a new consensus among honest scholars that King David really did exist.

The Merenptah Stele

> "Canaan has been plundered in every evil way, Askelon has been brought away captive, Gezer has been seized, Yenoam has been destroyed. Israel is devastated, having no seed."

The massive Merneptah Stele found at Luxor in 1896 now housed in the Cairo Museum.

This monument from the 19th Dynasty bears the oldest known reference to Israel, outside of the Bible.

Photo by Gerald Payton

These words are inscribed on a stone slab first found in 1896. The granite stele, uncovered by Sir Flinders Petrie, was first thought to be a memorial to the victories of Pharaoh Merenptah. However, recent analysis suggests that the king is simply recalling the victories of his father Rameses, his grandfather Seti, and their importance to the stability his kingdom was enjoying.

This ancient slab of black granite, now on display in the Cairo Museum has come to be known as the Israel Stele. It is called thusly because it contains the earliest reference to Israel found to date.

The designation of Israel on this monument is different than the others named. Found among the glyphs are determinatives. These determinatives are symbols that designate a word category, classifying Askelon, Gezer and Yanoam as cities. But the determinative for Israel indicates that *they are distinct people and not a geographic area.* Since the stele denotes Israel as a people, some Biblical scholars have tried to suggest this designation marks Merenptah as the Pharaoh of the Exodus. I have, hopefully, put that idea to rest in the main portions of this book.

The Sea Peoples

During one of my first visits to that vast vault of artifacts they call the Cairo Museum I saw a royal footstool. It immediately brought to mind the words of the Psalmist, *"The Lord said unto my lord, Sit thou at my right hand until I make thine enemies thy footstool."*[19] The stool was covered with illustrations of various warring peoples whose features made it obvious that they were not Egyptians. Their place on the footstool was also obvious. Prominently displayed among this rogue's gallery was a Philistine wearing the feathered headdress unique to his people. The Egyptians called them the *Peleshet*. They are also known as the Sea Peoples thanks to their sailing prowess and the location of their home base on the coastal plains that we now call Gaza.

Though they were distantly related to the Egyptians, through their ancestor Ham[20], the Philistines were a constant thorn in the side of the empire. To Israel these *Pulishtim* were an arch nemesis. David battled them for control of Canaan but we encounter them early on in the Biblical narrative when a Philistine monarch kidnaps Sarah, the wife of Abraham.[21]

On the banks of the Nile, near Luxor we can view a carved relief depicting the capture by Rameses the Third of the Philistines. Archaeological proof of the Philistines is one of the keystones in the quest to validate the historical accuracy of the Bible. The Minimalist camp argues that we cannot use the Bible as a research guide for archaeology. Remarkably, archaeologist Trudy Dothan points out, *"Without the Bible, we wouldn't even have known there were Philistines."*[22] Ms. Dothan is the recognized authority on the Philistines. She has dug extensively at Tel Ekron; a major site for Philistine occupation located a few miles east of present day Ashdod, on the coast of Israel.[23] Dothan's excavations, in association with Seymour Gitin, have unearthed a wealth of pottery, tools and even Philistine dwellings.[24]

The Moabite Stone

Carved on black basalt are the words of King Mesha, attributing his success in achieving independence from the kings who had ruled over his land. He attributes his triumph to his god *Kemosh.* The monument we now call the Moabite Stone or Mehsa Stele was shown to an Alsatian monk in 1868 and eventually taken to Jerusalem. It can now be seen in Paris in the Louvre.

The stele relates that Mesha rebelled against Ahab, the son of the Israelite King Omri. The latter had ruled the Northern Kingdom of Israel for twelve years followed by his son Ahab who sat on the throne for twenty-two years. One section of the stele's lengthy inscription reveals,

> "Omri was king of Israel, and he oppressed Moab for many days, for Kemosh was angry with his land. And his son succeeded him, and he said--he too--I will oppress Moab!"

The Second Book of Kings, in the third chapter, also gives an account of Mesha's rebellion against Israel after the death of King Ahab.[25]

There is another exciting aspect of the text on this monument that is generally ignored by most scholars and that is the reference to the Israelite tribe of Gad settling in Moab. A line on the stele reads,

> "And the men of Gad lived in the land of Atarot from ancient times."

These simple words, as dictated by the ancient King Mesha, directly point to the Biblical account of the people of Gad settling in the region just as described in the book Numbers, Chapter 32.[26] After conquering the region, which includes the aforementioned Atarot, the tribes of Gad and Reuben approach Moses and ask that they be allowed to settle there. Their request is granted and, just as described on the Mesha Stele, the book of Numbers tells us:

> "And the Children of Gad built Dibon and Atarot...."

This is the kind of tangible evidence that causes the Minimalists to tear at their collective hair. Klaas Smelik, a Professor of Old Testament Studies in Brussels, attests to its impact,

> "It should have become clear to the reader how important the Mesha stele is for the study of the Old Testament, as a historical source and as evidence of a religion which is closely related to that of Israel. This discovery is even so unique that several scholars have tried to show that it is a forgery....In fact, for Old Testament research this discovery is almost too good to be true."[27]

The Black Obelisk

In 1845, under the guidance of Henry Layard, workers digging the ruins of the ancient city of Calneh, near the Tigris River, unearthed an obelisk from the time of the Assyrian king Shalmanezer. A striking feature of this four-sided pillar is the relief depicting Israelites paying tribute to the Shalmanezer. Scholars agree that the spoils come from King Jehu. The text above the relief lists the gifts from Yahua which is Jehu:

> "Tribute of Yahua, son of Humri: I received silver, gold, a golden bowl, a golden beaker, golden pitchers, lead, a royal staff, a javelin.....[28]

Jehu was fifth in succession from Israel's King Omri but he was not directly related to him. Jehu, a commander from the tribe of Manasseh, took the Northern throne by force and ruled Israel from Samaria for twenty-eight years.[29] Though the Biblical text does not directly mention his dealings with an Assyrian monarch, the obelisk manages to both confirm Jehu as an historical figure and enlarge our knowledge of his reign outside of the Biblical account. The Assyrian armies that stormed down from Nineveh were always a threat. Years before Jehu took the throne, King Ahab and King Jehoshapat of Judah had allied to successfully thwart the Assyrians causing them to retreat across the Orontes River.[30]

Paying tribute was common in antiquity and enriched many a despot (in modern times, the Mafia did the same, extracting tribute and calling it "protection money"). The practice is found all through Biblical texts, for instance in the Chapter 17 of Second Kings we find:

> "Against the king came up Shalmaneser, king of Assyria; and Hoshea became his servant and gave him presents."

It was during the 9th year of Hoshea's rule that the Ten Tribes were taken captive by the Assyrian horde. That was about one hundred forty years after the time of Jehu. Layard's discovery of the Black Obelisk clearly conveys that Jehu was also being harassed by the Assyrians. Years later, Hoshea hoped to satisfy any lust for conquest on the part of Assyria by lavishing tribute but to no avail. It was during his reign that the Ten Northern Tribes of Israel were carried away by the Assyrians.[31]

The Taylor Prism

As we have already seen, the armies of their powerful neighbors to the North continually troubled the divided monarchy of Israel and Judah. The book of Second Chronicles also details this campaign which saw the army of Sennacherib surround the walls of ancient Jerusalem, locking the inhabitants inside. The despotic Sennacherib was the son of Sargon but believed that he could trace his ancestry back to mythical antediluvian hero *Gilgamesh*. He warred constantly in an attempt to enlarge the Assyrian holdings and his own fame. His ambitions were frustrated at Jerusalem.

Again, an ancient artifact offers us hard evidence of a Biblical event and it is of that failed campaign. The account is preserved on the so-called Taylor Prism. The relic is named for a Colonel Taylor who held the office of the British Resident in Baghdad. This fired clay record, obtained in 1830, makes direct reference to Hezekiah, king of Judah who Sennacherib says he shut up in the city, *"like a bird in a cage."*

The invader may have boasted of locking up Jerusalem but the Bible tells us that before Sennacherib's armies could enter the gates his forces were wiped out by catastrophe. Only the king survived to return home.[32] In his palace unearthed at Nineveh, on a sort of victory wall, are carved illustrations that recall his military incursion into Judah. His siege of Jerusalem is not found on any relief.

Why did Sennacherib fail to commemorate a total victory against Jerusalem? Maybe the oldest profession is actually "spin doctor" since it is characteristic of all monuments from the ancient Near East to diminish or deny the faults or disasters of the region's warring potentates. Historian C.W. Ceram reminds us that this is characteristic of tyrants past and present:

> "Indeed, the records of Sennacherib bring to mind the typically modern picture of a dictator shouting vast lies at vast audiences, civilian and military, confident in the knowledge that they will be swallowed whole."[33]

The Copper Scroll

Some readers will find this entry in our catalogue of Biblical proofs a controversial one. It is a discovery that has been dogged by debate since it was first uncovered in 1952. However, the Copper Scroll is an extraordinary link, not to the Second Temple, but to the First Temple period. The beginning of that era was unparalleled in the history of ancient Israel for pageantry and splendor. It was also a time of stability and peace as echoed in the name of its ruler, King Solomon; for the root of his name, *sholomo* is *shalom* or peace. Locating the holy treasures from the First Temple would mean finding the Ark of the Covenant and within it, the Tablets given to Moses on Mount Sinai.

The Copper Scroll is actually one of the Dead Sea Scrolls found in the same cave complex as its more famous counterparts. It is unique in several aspects. First of all, no other copper scroll has yet been found in Israel (it is hammered from the purest of copper). The other scrolls from Qumran are sacred books while this scroll is an inventory of holy treasures and their burial sites. With the exception of a few other parchment scraps, it is the only Dead Sea Scroll not in the possession of Israel. To this day, the Copper Scroll remains on display at the Museum of Antiquities in Amman, Jordan.

The unique Copper Scroll, found at Qumran in 1952, is now housed in the museum in Amman, Jordan.

Appendix A

Israel's 1948 War of Independence had already started when the first excavation teams converged on the caves at Qumran. After the area had been secured by Jordanian troops they allowed Professor Gerald Lankester Harding from the Jordanian Antiquities Authority and Father Roland De Vaux of Jerusalem's Ecole Biblique to excavate the site where the original Dead Sea Scrolls had been found. This was the beginning of the international scroll team whose ranks would swell to later include Father J.T. Milik, John Strugnell, John Allegro and others.[34]

The Copper Scroll was later discovered in Cave 3Q at Qumran by Muhammed Adh Dhib, the same Bedouin who is credited with finding the first seven Dead Sea Scrolls in 1947. Muhammed was digging for Professor Harding and paid only 15 Jordanian *dinar* for his efforts. At least that's what Adh Dhib told me when I videotaped an interview at the site of the original find in January of 1997.[35]

Apparently the initial discovery of the Copper Scroll created a lot of scholarly head scratching on the scroll team. John Allegro secured permission to transport the scroll to England where it was cut into twenty-three sheets at Manchester College of Science and Technology. Soon after, Father Milik was laboring over the text. The next response of Milik and the team, based on their understanding of the Copper Scroll's contents, seems typical of so many academics confronted with any archaeological anomaly. They simply dismissed this unusual document as a work of fiction.[36]

Though Allegro respected Milik's scholarship, he did not share his conclusion and launched a search in the spring of 1960 for the fabulous treasures listed in the Copper Scroll.[37] Allegro's hunt would prove fruitless but in the years since, the Copper Scroll has taken on a new luster of respect for scholars and it continues to be a subject of serious study. Many believed that the amount of gold and silver is genuine but that much of the wealth was from tithes to the Herodian Temple just before the Romans destroyed Jerusalem.[38]

The ravages of time are evident on this section of the Copper Scroll

Appendix A

A Texan, Professor Vendyl Jones, launched his own quest for the sacred riches of the Copper Scroll in 1967 as the smoke was clearing from the Six Day War. He had arrived just in time to serve as a volunteer observer. He happened to be color-blind. This visual aberration actually allowed him to detect the dyes used in camouflage and enabled him to pick out several enemy gun emplacements.[39]

Using the Copper Scroll as his guide, Jones began digging in the same cave complex at Qumran where the Bedouin first uncovered the original Dead Sea Scrolls in 1947. He had studied the translations as published by both Milik and Allegro but still decided to have a crack at deciphering the text of the Copper Scroll. He was at first intrigued by the lack of consistency in the inscriptions. Jones asked Professor Mary Williams, who taught handwriting analysis to police cadets, to examine the transcriptions of Copper Scroll text. She pointed out two details about the inscriptions: (1) that the scroll had been written in haste, possibly under stress and most importantly (2) there were five different handwriting styles. Jones wasn't sure how that information would aid him in his search so he mentally tucked it away for future reference.

Working with an Israeli-born translator, Jones was convinced that the ancient document was not only genuine but that the treasures listed in the Copper Scroll were from the First Temple, built by King Solomon. This belief has fueled the on-going work of Jones and his volunteers for over thirty years. That conviction was dramatically underscored when two young rabbis discovered a nearly forgotten work published in 1648 called *Emek Ha Melekh* (Valley of the King).

The book was the work of Rabbi Naphtali Hertz wherein he quotes *Tosephta* missing from the modern editions of the Talmud.[40] Rabbi Hertz tells of several *mishnayot* (records) that list a collection of holy treasures that were only found in the First Temple such as the Breastplate of Judgment, the Vestments of the High Priest and the Ark of the Covenant.[41] The Tabernacle itself is also found in this amazing catalog. Here is an important phrase found in Mishna 2:

> "These are the holy vessels and the vessels of the Temple that were in Jerusalem and in every place. They were inscribed by Shimor Ha Levi and his companions on a Copper Tablet…."[42]

Mishna 3 of the nearly forgotten tractates also revealed:

> "…These five men inscribed these mishnayot…"[43]

Two seemingly mundane items as referenced in *Emek Ha Melekh* and the *Tosephta* are key to linking the Copper Scroll to the First Temple period and the act of hiding its most awesome treasures. Unless another copper scroll is found, this fragile metal document seems to be the most likely candidate for the "copper tablet" mentioned in *Emek Ha Melekh*. It does tell of massive amounts gold and silver and it was the handiwork of five different authors. This is a subject ripe for further exploration but needless to say, discovering the treasures of the Copper Scroll would impact the nation of Israel and ultimately the world.

In listing each of the previous discoveries, I have tried to suggest a chronological order. It is my attempt to draw the reader along a path littered with physical testimony strongly suggesting that the pivotal events and characters of the Bible not only existed but left a trail etched across time in stone and clay.

Notes to Appendix A

[1] E.W. Faulstich, *History, Harmony, The Exile & Return*, pp. 16-17 (Chronology Books 1988)

[2] 2Kings 15:30 (KJV)[1] The magazine's 2001 January/February issue listed 28 dig sites.

[3] The magazines's 2001 January/February issue listed 28 dig sites.

[4]Joshua 11:1-13

[5] David Briggs, *Archaeologists Unearth Evidence of Biblical Occurrences* , Associated Press, Ft.Worth Star-Telegram/ Friday, December 20, 1996

[6] Michael D. Lemonick, *Are the Bible's Stories True?* (Time Magazine, Dec 18, 1995)

[7] Numbers 22:5

[8] Deuteronomy 27:3-4

[9] Klass A.D. Smelik, *Writings from Ancient Israel*, (Westminster/ John Knox Press 1991)

[10] John Garstang, *Joshua Judges*, pp.144-146

[9]11Bryant Wood, *Did the Israelites Conquer Jericho*?, Biblical Archaeology Review (March/April 1990)

[12] ibid

[13] David Rohl, *Pharaohs and Kings*, pp.195-219 (Crown, NYC 1995)

[14] ibid

[15] from the Hebrew root *shakhan* which means "to dwell."

[16] Ian Wilson, *The Bible is History*, pp. 108-109, (Weidnefeld & Nicolson 1999)

[17] Michael D. Lemonick, *Are the Bible's Stories True?* (Time Magazine, Dec 18, 1995)

[18] David Briggs, *Archaeologists Unearth Evidence of Biblical Occurrences*, (Associated Press /Ft.Worth-Star Telegram, 12/20/96)

[19] Psalms 110:1

[20] Genesis 10:6-14

[21] Genesis 20:2

[22] *Mysteries of Faith*, U.S. News & World Report Special Collector's Edition (2001), p.3

[23] 1Samuel 7:14

[24] Ian Wilson, *The Bible is History*, pp. 96-99 (Weidenfeild & Nicolson, UK 1999)

[25] 2Kings 3:4

[26] Numbers 32:2 & Numbers 32:34

[27] Klaas A.D. Smelik, *Writings from Ancient Israel* (Westminster/ John Knox Press 1991)

[28] Alan Millard, *Treasures from Bible Times*, pp.119-120 (Lion Publishing 1985)

[29] 2Kings 9:4-23 details Jehu's bloody path to the throne of Israel. Among those who died during his rampage was the infamous Jezebel, the Baal-worshipping queen of King Ahab.

[30] Monroe Rosenthal & Isaac Mozeson, *Wars of the Jews*, pp.57-58 (Hippocrene Books 1990)

[31] 2Kings 17:1-3

[32] 2Kings 18:13-19:36

[33] C.W. Ceram, *Gods, Graves and Scholars*, p.269 (Alfred A. Knopf 1966)

[34] Lawrence H. Schiffman, *Reclaiming the Dead Sea Scrolls*, pp.6-11 (Doubleday 1995)

[35] It should be noted that there are others who claim to be Adh Dhib. One of these passed away in Jordan, in 1994. According to a Jerusalem Post article, dated August 2, 1997, this particular Adh Dhib believed that a *jinn* (evil spirit) had cursed him for life because he disturbed the cave containing the Dead Sea Scrolls.

[36] John Marco Allegro, *The Treasure of the Copper Scroll*, pp.29-38, (Anchor Books 1964)

[37] Schiffman, p.15

[38] P. Kyle McCarter, *Mystery of the Copper Scroll* from *Understanding the Dead Sea Scrolls* edited by Herschel Shanks, p. 240-241, (Random House 1992)

[39] Time Magazine, p.18, June 16, 1967

[40] A collection of early rabbinic commentaries or additions to the *Mishna*

[41] Vendyl Jones, *The Copper Scroll & the Excavations at Qumran* (Vendyl Jones Research Institutes 1995)

[42] Ibid

[43] Ibid

APPENDIX B

The Splintered Reed

> "Look—you're relying on that splintered reed of a staff, Egypt, which enters one's hand and pierces it if he leans on it! That's what King Pharaoh of Egypt is like for anyone who relies on him" - Isaiah 36:6

Shishak/Shoshank

Long after the Exodus, Israel would variously clash or coexist with the Egyptian empire. While we find the acts of various pharaohs recorded in the sacred text, we can also find those same rulers listed in the Egypt annals.

The wise Solomon was the first Israelite king to make an alliance with a pharaoh of Egypt. He sealed the deal by marrying the daughter of the Pharaoh and later building a house for her in Jerusalem.[1] This is most likely the same Egyptian ruler who would later gave political asylum to Solomon's adversary, Jeroboam. Chapter 11 of 1st Kings, verse 40 calls this pharaoh Shishak. Most Biblical scholars believe that this is *Shoshank I*, a 22nd Dynasty king who attacked Ayilon, Gibeon, Bethshan, Meggido and many other sites all over Israel.

He commemorated that campaign on a wall still found at Karnak today. That massive military incursion is also believed to be the same as the action related in the Chapter 14 of 1st Kings. During the reign of Rehoboam, the son of Solomon, pharaoh Shishak attacked Jerusalem. He was allowed to loot the storehouse of the Temple in exchange for sparing the city.[2]

I want to briefly address the misconception that Pharaoh Shishak took the Ark of the Covenant during this campaign. This notion is often aided by a less than accurate rendering of the Hebrew word *otsar* as "treasures". The word should actually be translated "storehouse" of the Temple. Our word "store" comes from this same root *oTSar*. While the text also takes pains to note that several golden shields are taken, there is no mention of the most sacred objects being looted.

In fact, the *only* time that the Ark ever fell into enemy hands is after the Philistines defeat the Israelites at Aphek. The Bible gives an exhaustive account, running for several chapters in 1st Samuel, detailing how the Philistines transport the Ark to their Dagon temple at Ashdod and possess it for seven months.[3] If Shishak had stolen the Ark of God, surely the text would not remain silent about such a tragic event.

Egyptologist Sir Alan Gardiner made a valid connection between Shishak and Shoshank,

> "However, the discovery at Meggido of a fragment mentioning Shoshenk leaves no doubt as to the reality of his campaign..."[4]

David Rohl admits that the name of this historical figure can sometimes be found written without the 'n' hieroglyph. However, he still argues that this pharaoh is not the Biblical Shishak simply because the name is also spelled with the added 'n'.[5] I would not disqualify

Typical of the reliefs found at Karnak and Luxor depicting bound captives. At Karnak, a relief names Biblical cities captured during the campaign of Pharaoh Shoshank.

Shoshank as the Biblical Shishak on this basis. When a name like Shishak is spoken aloud, the 'n' sound is sometimes added due to a common linguistic phenomenon called "nasalization". The linguistic question is really a minor compared to the problem Rohl has with the massive display at Karnak that herald's the triumphs of Shoshank in Israel. Though the relief reads like a bus schedule of ancient Israel, Rohl claims that the name of Jerusalem is not among the defeated cities and because of that, he wants to believe that Shoshank and Shishak cannot be the same pharaoh.

This question can be resolved by consulting 2nd Chronicles, Chapter 12. We learn that Shishak invades the land of Israel, looting and pillaging his way to Jerusalem. The language of the Biblical account clearly indicates that pharaoh successfully takes every site he attacks. However, that same text reveals that Jerusalem does not fall when King Jeroboam and his advisers pray to God for deliverance. Jerusalem is spared.

"Whereupon the princes of Israel and the king humbled themselves; and they said, The LORD *is* righteous. And when the LORD saw that they humbled themselves, the word of the LORD came to Shemaiah, saying, They have humbled themselves; *therefore* I will not destroy them, but I will grant them some deliverance; and my wrath shall not be poured out upon Jerusalem by the hand of Shishak. Nevertheless they shall be his servants; that they may know my service, and the service of the kingdoms of the countries."[6]

Clearly the Biblical record shows that Shishak was allowed to plunder the Temple stores. In this way the capitol city of Jerusalem is spared the same fate as the surrounding cities of Judah. Had King Rehoboam been taken captive he surely would have been found among the other 28 chieftains who are shown as a bound prisoners on the wall at Karnak. The account in 1 Kings and 2nd Chronicles makes it evident that Rehoboam was not taken captive.

One of the vast halls of the Cairo Museum. This massive repository contains thousands of archaeological treasures from Egypt's past

Tirhakha/Taharq

During part of the 25th Dynasty, an Ethiopian known as Taharq who is clearly the Biblical Tirhakha, a contemporary of King Hezekiah, ruled the southern region of Egypt from Thebes.[7] Meanwhile, the northern capital of Memphis was subject to the occupied forces of Assyria. The northern nomes, or districts, were under the rule of Sennacherib and then his son, Esarhaddon.

Necho

Another Pharaoh found in the Bible and the Egyptian annals is Necho. He is directly connected to the death of the heroic King Josiah. Historians refer to this rather ambitious pharaoh as Necho II. He is credited with building canals and dispatching mariners around the Mediterranean. He also marched on Assyria and the emerging Babylonian empire. On his way north he met resistance from King Josiah.[8]

> "...Neco king of Egypt went up to fight at Carchemish on the Euphrates, and Josiah marched out to meet him in battle. But Neco sent messengers to him, saying, "What quarrel is there between you and me, O king of Judah? It is not you I am attacking at this time, but the house with which I am at war. God has told me to hurry; so stop opposing God, who is with me, or he will destroy you."[9]

King Josiah, the last righteous king of Judah, was slain by the archers of Pharaoh Necho. The Egyptian ruler marched on to Carchemish and victory. Necho later deposed Josiah's son, Jehoahz, and installed his older brother on the throne of Judah. The pharaoh also fined the treasury in Jerusalem and changed the king's name from Eliakim to Jehoiakim just to demonstrate his authority.[10]

Hophra

The downfall of Judah's King Zedekiah at the hands of Nebuchadnezzar was precipitated because of Zedekiah's political alliance with Pharaoh Hophra. The prophet Jeremiah warned that such an alliance went against the will of God, and told Hophra that he would suffer much the same fate as Zedekiah.

> "God says: I will deliver King Pharaoh Chophra of Egypt into the hands of his enemies, who seek his life, just as I delivered King Zedekiah of Judah into the hands of his enemy, King Nebuchadnezzar of Babylon, who sought his life."[11]

In the Egyptian annals he is Uah-ab-Ra, but the Greeks called him Apries. On paper, these names appear to be different, but when vocalized they sound alike. Whatever you call this ruler, the warnings of Jeremiah would prove tragically prophetic for the pharaoh. According to Herodotus, Hophra's own army revolted against him. They imprisoned and then strangled him.[12]

Notes on Appendix B

[1] 1Kings 3:1, also see 1Kings 9:16 (KJV)

[2] 1Kings 14:25 (KJV)

[3] 1Sam. 4:1 through 1Sam 7:1 (KJV)

[4] Sir Alan Gardiner, *Egypt of the Pharaohs*, p.330 (Oxford University Press 1961)

[5] David Rohl, *Pharaohs and Kings*, p.128 (Crown Publishers 1995)

[6] 2Chronicles 12:1-10 (KJV)

[7] 2Kings 19:19 and Isaiah 37:9 (KJV)

[8] Ernest A. Wallis Budge, *The Mummy*, pp. 56-57 (Senate 1995)

[9] 2Chronicles 35:20 (KJV)

[10] 2Chronicles 36:3 (KVJ)

[11] Jeremiah 44:30 (The Living 'Nach, Moznaim Publishers)

[12] Heinrich Brugsch-Bey, *Egypt Under the Pharaohs*, p445-446 (Bracken Books 1996)

INDEX

A

B

C

D

E

G